Helen N.   19.99

GW01019515

Business English Pair Work

Steven Flinders and Simon Sweeney

Illustrated by Neville Swaine

SERIES EDITOR: NICK BRIEGER

In memory of Frank Zappa (1940–93)

PENGUIN BOOKS

PENGUIN BOOKS

Published by the Penguin Group
Penguin Books Ltd, 27 Wrights Lane, London W8 5TZ, England
Penguin Books USA Inc., 375 Hudson Street, New York, New York 10014, USA
Penguin Books Australia Ltd, Ringwood, Victoria, Australia
Penguin Books Canada Ltd, 10 Alcorn Avenue, Toronto, Ontario, Canada M4V 3B2
Penguin Books (NZ) Ltd, 182–190 Wairau Road, Auckland 10, New Zealand

Penguin Books Ltd, Registered Offices: Harmondsworth, Middlesex, England

Published by Penguin Books 1996
10 9 8 7 6 5 4 3 2 1

Text copyright © Steven Flinders and Simon Sweeney 1996
Illustrations copyright © Neville Swaine 1996
All rights reserved

The moral right of the authors and of the illustrator has been asserted

Illustrations by Neville Swaine

Every effort has been made to trace copyright holders in every case. The publishers
would be interested to hear from any not acknowledged here

Printed in England by William Clowes Limited, Beccles and London
Set in New Century Schoolbook by Goodfellow & Egan, Cambridge

Except in the United States of America, this book is sold subject to the condition that it
shall not, by way of trade or otherwise, be lent, resold, hired out, or otherwise circulated
without the publisher's prior consent in any form of binding or cover other than that in
which it is published and without a similar condition including this condition being
imposed on the subsequent purchaser

Acknowledgements

The authors are especially grateful to Peter Watcyn-Jones who developed the pair work
concept in his book *Pair Work*, also published by Penguin. We also thank friends and
colleagues at York Associates, Paul Smith and Conny Montague of Paul Smith Associates
in Germany for an idea developed in Activity 8, Business gifts; Robert Townsend, author
of *Up the Organisation* (Coronet Books, 1970), for some of the suggestions in Activity
17, Corporate culture; Marcus Child of Pilgrim's Executive Language Centre,
Canterbury, the originator of the idea in Activity 56, Small talk; TMS Development
International Ltd., 128 Holgate Road, York YO2 4DL, for permission to reproduce the
Team Management Wheel and brief role descriptions in Activity 59, Team building.

Thanks too to Nick Brieger who edited the text and made many apt criticisms and
suggestions and also to colleagues at Penguin.

The authors and the publisher also wish to thank the following people and organizations
who gave permission to use various illustrations: Activity 2: © Tony Stone Images/Phil
Cole; Activity 37: © Greg Evans International/M. Wells; Activity 44: © Robert Harding
Picture Library/Warren Morgan.

Contents

Introduction

To the teacher

Business English Pair Work has been designed to give foreign students of Business English, working in pairs, further classroom practice in communicative activities in order to develop fluency in communication skills. The material addresses a wide range of themes from a variety of professional areas; however, most of the activities do not require specialist knowledge.

The activities have been designed in order to provide communicative practice around:

- business communication skills
- key language functions.

The material is completely independent of any course book and can, therefore, be used on any Business English course.

Business English Pair Work consists of sixty-five activities. The activities are in one book containing:

- teachers' notes
- the role information for student **A**
- the role information for student **B**
- a glossary of business terms
- an A–Z of language functions together with sample exponents
- a table showing the communication skill(s) practised in each activity.

Target learners

The activities are aimed at learners of Business English at intermediate level or above. All the activities can be done by in-service learners: people who need English for their work. Most of the activities can also be done in their existing form by pre-service learners: people training for a career in the business world. The few remaining activities can be done by pre-service learners after minor adaptations have been made and explanations of key concepts have been given by the teacher. The teachers' notes provide suggestions for lead-in activities to get pre-service students thinking about business management areas; the glossary provides key words for the management areas covered.

Description and organization

The book contains sixty-five pair work activities. These are arranged in alphabetical order by title (see contents page), except for the Ice breaker, which comes first. The activities can be done in any order, and roles **A** and **B** can be taken by either person in the pair. All the information for each activity is given in the book. Each activity consists of:

- a short introduction to set the scene and provide some background information about the business theme

- Student **A**'s role (first part of the book)
- Student **B**'s role (second part of the book).

Each activity focuses on a communication skill (see below). Therefore, we have shown for each activity:

- the communication skill to be practised
- the language function(s) which may be drawn out.

All of the activities can be done in pairs; however, some of the discussion activities can also be done in small groups.

Activity types

There are four main types of activity in the book.

Information gap:
These are activities in which students are asked to perform a task together; they fall into two types. In the first, one student has access to all the information and tries to impart it to his/her partner. In the second, both students are given access to half the information and by working together try to solve the whole.

Discussion and conversation:
These are activities designed to stimulate students to discuss a subject or subjects with their partners, usually in order to reach agreement. These activities can often be done in small groups as well as by pairs.

Role play:
These are activities in which students are given specific roles to play in order to carry out a task.

Simulation:
These are activities in which students play themselves but are given a definite task to do or are put in a specific situation.

Communication skills

By doing the activities, students will practise:

- presentations
- phone calls
- meetings and discussions
- negotiations
- social English in a professional context.

The materials are designed both to practise communication skills and develop effective communication techniques. Thus they focus on both fluency and effect-iveness.

How to use the book

The activities are not graded and can be done in any order. You can choose an activity on the basis of theme or communication skill.

Suggested procedure for the activity

1 Present the overall theme of the activity, focusing on key vocabulary for the topic.

2 Warm up class with lead-in questions in teachers' notes; focus on key vocabulary that will be needed in the activity.

3 Divide the class into pairs.

4 Assign roles **A** and **B**.

5 Ask students to read the introduction.

6 Ask students to look at the information for their role. Make sure that they know what they have to do and, if necessary, how long they have to do it.

7 Give students enough time to prepare. This is particularly important for some of the activities, where students need both to absorb and understand the information before starting to communicate.

8 Monitor the pairs while they carry out the activity, prompting the use of functional exponents, if necessary.

Suggested procedure after the activity

1 Feedback to the learner(s). Provide feedback for individuals, pairs, or the class on strengths and weaknesses, appropriate usage and/or mistakes. Refer students to glossary for vocabulary items, where appropriate.

2 Feedback from the learner(s). For problem-solving activities, ask pairs to present their solutions. One technique which involves the whole class is as follows:

a) ask one pair to repeat the activity with another pair

b) ask one group of four to repeat the activity with another group

c) enlarge the group size each time, until a joint conclusion has been reached.

3 Follow-up activities. The teachers' notes provide ideas for follow-up activities which can be done either in class or for homework.

Timing

Some activities can be short (about 10 minutes); others are likely to take longer, perhaps even a whole lesson. There are no time limits on the activities, except those decided by the teacher and the learners. However, you should agree and set time limits – both for the preparation and the activity. Don't allow an activity to drag on too long. Better a few minutes too short than too long.

Additional resources

As some of the activities involve figures, a pocket calculator may be useful.

Teachers' notes

1 Ice breaker

Introduction
'Ice breakers' are short exercises for use with a new class to help people to get to know each other.

Lead-in
Ask why it is important for business people to be able to:
- 'break the ice' with strangers
- ask polite questions to find out more about business contacts
- be able to say clearly and concisely who they are, what they do and where they come from.

Method
- With a group class, divide students into As and Bs. There are two possible methods. Either Bs ask all their questions, then As question Bs. Or students take it in turns to ask a question.
- If the group is not too large, get students to walk around so that all the As interview all the Bs and vice versa.

Follow-up
1 Get selected students to tell the whole group in one or two sentences:
   - their name
   - their job title and main responsibility
   - their company, company activity (if necessary) and company location.

   You may wish to provide a model, for example: 'My name is Sylvia Smith and I'm a language trainer responsible for business English training at ABC Pharmaceuticals, based in Berlin.'

   Explain that this is a vital skill which everyone in the group must be able to perform with ease by the end of the course. If some students are unsure about their job titles, get others to make suggestions. If uncertainty persists in any case, suggest that both you and the student try to get more information before your next meeting.
2 Get students to write short personal and professional profiles of their partners, for example as in a job application form.

2 Advertising

Introduction
This role play revolves around how to allocate money available for advertising.

Lead-in
Questions:
- what methods of advertising are there?
- what methods would be suitable for advertising sports equipment?

Method
1 Direct student **A** to state an initial position. **B** should respond with some general comments and observations – on football sponsorship, for example. **A** needs to choose between a broadly-based package centred on athletics sponsorship, or a narrower campaign led by TV advertising. Student **B** has to change **A**'s mind – away from football sponsorship.
2 Make sure learners come to an agreement on a total package and that all points in their roles are included in the discussion.

Follow-up
After giving feedback, noting the positive achievements of the negotiation, suggest an exchange of letters summarizing the agreement.

3 Agendas

Introduction
The activity involves a discussion on the telephone about planning an agenda for a meeting.

Lead-in
1 Discuss the theme of quality:
   - what is quality?
   - how do companies raise and maintain quality standards?
2 Then elicit comments on agendas:
   - should all business meetings have agendas?
   - are written agendas always necessary?
   - the answer could be that all meetings need clear objectives, but they may not always be written down.

Method

1 After the introductory discussion above, students prepare their roles and **B** starts, reminding **A** about his/her letter and making some general critical remarks together with suggestions.
2 They should reach agreement on a new agenda but postpone some discussion to the meeting itself. Note that the final agenda depends on other people's comments too.

Follow-up

They should produce a new agenda together.

4   Bank charges

Introduction

This activity is essentially about customer service in a familiar context: a bank.

Lead-in

1 Ask students to discuss what they think of banks and the quality of service they provide. They may recall some personal experiences, good and not so good.
2 Move discussion on to the nature of customer service and why the concept is important.

Method

A begins the role play by ringing with a complaint. **B** has to decide how to respond. The role play is potentially highly conflictive, much depending on how student **B**, the bank employee, decides to resolve the two problems involved. There are several possible ways to resolve the difficulties, depending on the bank's keenness to provide a customer-friendly service.

Follow-up

Have students work together to create a short dialogue based on handling a complaint to a bank. Reverse the roles so **B** is making the complaint. Alternatively get them to change the context from banking to another service industry.

5 Budget presentation

Introduction

The activity provides practice in presenting information and in listening to a presentation and asking for explanations.

Lead-in

Check students' understanding of key vocabulary, such as *budget*, *sales budget*, *cost of sales* and *cost of selling*.

Method

Explain the two roles – **A** as presenter, **B** as a listener who needs to understand precisely what **A** is saying and to question any part of the budget that is not totally clear.

Follow-up

Some learners may choose to present some other information relating to their own work or interests and invite questions from their partners. This would be a good opportunity to reverse the roles of presenter and listener.

6 Business anecdote

Introduction

This activity can be used to finish off a lesson or a course, or as a break between two more extended, intensive activities.

Lead-in

Is it important for business people to be able to tell anecdotes? Why is it important for business people to be able to tell them clearly and CONCISELY?

Method

1 Tell students that there are six stages. Tell them how long you would like them to spend on each one. (1–1$\frac{1}{2}$ minutes per stage.)
2 Signal to students when the time for each stage is up. Be firm about the changeover.
3 Listen in to each pair. Be ready to prompt students who have difficulty coming up with ideas.
4 When the exercise is over, get students, still in pairs, to go over the story again in order to improve and polish it.
5 Invite selected pairs to report their stories to the whole group.

Follow-up

1 Get students in pairs to tell each other their own business anecdotes. Get partners to report back to the group the anecdotes they have just heard. Again, encourage clarity and conciseness at every stage.
2 Get students to write down the anecdote they have invented or their own anecdote.
3 Language analysis and feedback.

7 Business etiquette

Introduction

This activity encourages students to reflect upon everyday business behaviour, to formulate rules for their own behaviour, and to learn about the rules governing other people's behaviour.

Lead-in

What aspects of business etiquette are important in the students' own culture? What happens if you break the rules?

Method

1 Every student has five different areas to cover. Tell **A**s and **B**s that they are going to take it in turns to describe certain aspects of business behaviour to each other.

2 **A**s and **B**s should read their copies. Give them a little time to think about the rules governing their own behaviour for each area listed on their own sheets.

3 Get **A**s to lead with *Shaking hands*. **A**s tell **B**s what the conventions for shaking hands are in their country/company/department as appropriate. **B**s should then comment on the differences between what **A**s have described and their own experience.

4 Get **B**s to do the same with *Business cards* and continue alternation until the end.

Follow-up

1 General reporting back. Get each **A** to report on a **B** area and vice versa, leading into general discussion.

2 Invite opinions about other areas of everyday business life, for example, punctuality, the status of deadlines, smoking at work.

3 Ask whether any of these areas are codified or whether any of them should be.

---

8 Business gifts

Introduction

The activity is based on an internal discussion to formulate policy on employees receiving gifts from suppliers or customers.

Lead-in

To introduce the theme, ask:

- what is the purpose of business gifts?
- are gifts common in your country?
- can they cause problems or conflict?
- what sort of things could be presented as gifts?

Method

Students should engage in a wide-ranging discussion, bringing in all the points on their role cards. Get them to reach a generally agreed new policy on gifts.

Follow-up

A jointly produced memo stating company policy on receiving gifts.

---

9 Business initials

Introduction

Like the quizzes, this can be treated as a quite light-hearted exercise to round off a lesson or a course. There is nevertheless a serious and useful pedagogical objective. It is important for business people to be able to read the international business press. Unfamiliar sets of initials are often a barrier to understanding when reading in a foreign language. This activity includes some of the more common sets of initials from the worlds of business, politics, economics, computing, etc.

Method

1 Get **B**s to test **A**s on sets of initials 1–16. **B**s should give the correct answer after each attempt by **A**s; where necessary they should explain each answer as far as they can, and score their partners out of 16.

2 Now reverse roles and get **A**s to test **B**s.

3 Pairs report back to the group with teacher clarifying any remaining problem sets. Ask students if their company has a VP for HR or R&D, what their company's USP is, or whether their company runs a TQA programme.

Follow-up

1 Ask students to provide their own sets of initials in English to test the rest of the class.

2 Provide newspapers/news magazines for the group and ask them to identify either as many sets of initials as possible from the quiz; or other sets of initials for further quiz work.

Answers

MD   Managing Director. The manager with overall responsibility for the day-to-day running of the company (British English).

VP   Vice-President. Usually with a departmental or geographical responsibility, for example: Vice-President in charge of Human Resources or Vice-President Sales, Central and South American Region (American English).

R&D   Research and Development. The division of a company doing the technical or scientific work needed to find new products.

PA   Personal Assistant. A senior executive's helper. PAs are usually thought to be more than secretaries but less than managers.

Teachers' notes

MBA   Master in Business Administration. The most important business school or university qualification in business. Some students do the MBA straight after their first degree; others get a few years' job experience first.

EU   European Union. The political and economic group whose current members are Austria, Belgium, Denmark, Eire, Finland, France, Germany, Greece, Netherlands, Italy, Luxembourg, Portugal, Spain, Sweden and the United Kingdom.

GATT   General Agreement on Tariffs and Trade. The main international free trading agreement between nations, aiming to reduce as far as possible the barriers to trade across national frontiers. The most recent GATT was eventually signed in 1994 after lengthy negotiations known as the Uruguay Round.

IBM   International Business Machines. Still the world's biggest computer company.

SAS   Scandinavian Airline Systems. The airline company for the Nordic countries.

WP   Word Processing. Typing and editing text on a computer.

RAM   Random Access Memory. The dynamic system memory of a computer that holds programmes and data while they are being worked on.

AGM   Annual General Meeting. The meeting, for example, of a company's shareholders, which takes place once a year.

GNP   Gross National Product. The measure of the wealth created by a country in a year, including money earned from abroad.

VAT   The general tax applied at each point of exchange of goods or services.

The 4 Ps   Price, Promotion, Packaging, Place. These are the main components of the Marketing Mix, the most important factors in the marketing of a product.

ILO   International Labour Organization. A United Nations Agency concerned with the rights, protection and health and safety of workers worldwide.

CEO   Chief Executive Officer. The manager with overall responsibility for the day-to-day running of the company. (More commonly used in American English).

VIP   Very Important Person. Rich, famous, or powerful people who receive special treatment. Major airports, for example, often have a VIP lounge.

HR   Human Resources. The management of such things as pay and conditions for all people who work in a company.

PR   Public Relations. The job of Public Relations is to ensure that the public image of a company is as positive as possible.

PhD   Doctor of Philosophy. The doctorate can, however, be in any of a wide range of subjects, not just philosophy.

ECU   European Currency Unit. A currency which is an average of a certain number of other European currencies and possibly the future single currency for all the members of the European Union (EU).

OECD   Organization for Economic Cooperation and Development. An economic research and forecasting agency funded by the rich industrialized nations and based in Paris, whose aim is to encourage economic growth, high employment and financial stability among its members.

ABB   Asea Brown Boveri. A major Swiss-Swedish engineering company.

JAL   Japan Airlines. The main Japanese airline company.

DTP   Desk Top Publishing. The computer-based activity which produces text with integrated graphics and varied layout, for example for a newsletter, CV or home-produced magazine.

CPU   Central Processing Unit. The brain of a computer.

AOB   Any Other Business. The last item on the agenda of a meeting.

GDP   Gross Domestic Product. The measure of the wealth created by a country in a year, excluding money earned from abroad.

USP   Unique Selling Proposition. What every company should have – a unique reason why customers should buy from them rather than from any other.

TQA   Total Quality Assurance. An approach to seeking to achieve the highest quality of product or service provided by getting everyone in the organization to focus on quality all the time.

IMF   International Monetary Fund. A fund set up in 1947 and to which most of the countries in the world belong, which exists to lend money to countries in financial difficulties, particularly to help with balance of payments problems. The IMF often withholds loans to governments if it does not approve of their economic policy plans.

10 Buying and selling

Introduction
Negotiation is an important skill not only for people involved in the kind of lengthy discussion needed, for example, to set up this kind of agency agreement; but also in informal everyday situations like persuading someone to stay on late at work or changing a holiday date. This activity can be useful practice for both formal or large-scale negotiation and informal or small-scale negotiation.

Lead-in
In what situations are negotiating skills necessary? Are these skills relevant only in the workplace?

Method
1 Give students plenty of time to read their activity sheets. Calculators could be useful.
2 Set a clear time limit – 20 or 25 minutes should be enough – for the activity, and give students two or three minutes' warning before you stop them.
3 Get students to start with some small talk before going into the main body of the negotiation.
4 Get each pair to summarize the main points of their agreement so that each participant is clear about what has been agreed.

Follow-up
1 Get selected pairs to talk through the stages in their negotiation in order to analyse the reasons for their particular result.
2 Get students to write down the terms of their agreement.

11 Cashflow problems

Introduction
The activity is a fairly complex face-to-face discussion between a cautious finance manager and an ambitious marketing manager reluctant to turn away a major order.

Lead-in
As a lead-in, discuss the meaning, causes and implications of cashflow problems.

Method
1 Both sides need a few minutes to prepare their roles and absorb the information they have.
2 **B** should start by outlining the order and asking how much cash is available. **A** is pessimistic about the cashflow situation.

3 In discussion, both sides need to reach agreement on exactly what is possible and what steps need to be taken next.

Follow-up
1 Together both students could work out a letter to the customer offering a unit price discount but requesting tight payment terms.
2 They could also work out a revised cash budget on the basis of the order and a possible bank loan.

12 Company of the year

Introduction
This activity can help students to focus, albeit in a potentially lighthearted way, on the perennial problem of how to make small businesses grow. If necessary, the situation could be adapted to the context of a department or profit centre if participants all work in large organizations.

Lead-in
In what situations are companies given prizes? What type of prizes are given? What companies have won prizes?

Method
1 If you suspect that students may not be very forthcoming about imagining their own company into existence, brainstorm an example with the whole class before the activity begins.
2 Note that the list of preferences for **A** and **B** are different.

Follow-up
During feedback, find out what the students' own ideas were and list them on the board. See whether any pattern emerges from the choices made by the different pairs.

13 Company organization

Introduction
The activity is based on a face-to-face discussion where both sides need to resolve a problem: how to design a new organization for their companies who are planning to merge.

Lead-in
Start by asking:
• why companies have hierarchies
• why companies have structured organization
• if there are alternatives to traditional company structures.

Method
- Each side needs to explain its primary objectives and to outline its concerns. There will be some trade off between the two.
- Students can sit side by side and actually draw up a fresh organization chart based on their preferred options and what they can agree on.

Follow-up
A joint presentation of the new structure using a board or OHP.

14 Company presentation

Introduction
Introducing oneself and one's work is a common communication need in international business. This activity gives an opportunity to practise a relatively formal presentation.

Lead-in
To introduce the theme, discuss the function of trade fairs and what goes on at such events.

Method
This is a two-part activity in which students both present a fictitious company and hear about one.
1 Ask **A** to present Conta Inc. **B** interrupts with requests for clarification and/or further information. **B** can also take notes.
2 Next, **B** presents Edile S.p.A. and the roles are therefore reversed.

Follow-up
Ask learners to present their own or another real company that they know well. Suggest they include saying who they are and what their responsibilities are. A further follow-up is to try a similar presentation, but much more informally.

15 Company tour

Introduction
It is important for business people to be able to talk clearly and concisely about their company's products, history and organization, as well as being able to guide visitors round the workplace.

Lead-in
Which companies receive visitors? Are there any special security arrangements? Are there any special risks about showing visitors around?

Method
1 The notes below the plan on **A**'s sheet are only brief guidelines for **A**, who will need time to prepare the presentation. The preparation could be done before the lesson.
2 Encourage **B**s to prepare lots of questions so that the activity is as interactive as possible. Discourage monologues from **A**s.

Follow-up
1 Repeat the activity with the roles reversed.
2 Get **A**s and **B**s to write follow-up letters to the visit:
   – **A**s saying they are hoping for business from **B**s
   – **B**s saying whether or not they have decided to do business with **A**s.

16 Company visit

Introduction
This is an information gap exercise which also provides practice in numbers and spelling and checking information. It can thus be used with lower level students.

Lead-in
Ask the students if:
- they have any problems with spelling foreign names
- they have any problems with understanding numbers
- if they have any special strategies for spelling and counting.

Method
1 Get students to write down any information, e.g. car registration or telephone numbers, that they give to their partners.
2 At the end of the activity, get students to check that all the information has been correctly transferred.

Follow-up
Repeat the activity with the roles reversed. Partners now know what information they have to give so should give a more polished performance.

17 Corporate culture

Introduction
The main aim of this activity is to provoke discussion so don't be too concerned if the students fail to come up with a coherent policy by the time you call the group together.

Lead-in

Ask students if they know any companies with their own special culture. What are the characteristics of corporate culture? Does it help employees to work better together?

Method

Encourage students to add ideas in the same spirit to the list.

Follow-up

1 In the group discussion following the activity, get students to identify the assumptions underlying the various possible policies on the list, e.g. that companies are too hierarchical, that there are not enough women in top management, etc. and find out if they agree with these assumptions or not. Which ones do they think are nonsensical? Why?
2 Get the group to brainstorm their own equally unorthodox policy suggestions.

18 Corporate sponsorship

Introduction

The activity is designed to encourage extensive discussion. Students may wish to invent details of the company they both represent and such details may influence the final choice. Otherwise, there is no obviously right answer.

Lead-in

Why do companies offer sponsorship? What types of events do they sponsor? What benefits does each side get?

Method

Since this activity involves quite a lot of reading, allow time for this before beginning the activity or distribute the activity sheets before the lesson begins.

Follow-up

1 Systematize feedback from the group by asking for the strong and the weak points of each file and writing them up on the board.
2 Get students to write a letter of acceptance to the sponsorship recipient and of rejection to the other two causes.

19 Costs and reducing overheads

Introduction

The activity involves a fairly detailed face-to-face

negotiation in which each participant will have to compromise in order to reach the desired objective. See also Activity 27 on franchising.

Lead-in

To introduce the theme, check students' understanding of *costs*, *cost of sales* and *cost of selling*.

Method

Each player in the negotiation approaches the problem from a rather different perspective: **A** is more conservative in terms of defending employees' interests, while **B** is more inclined to defend shareholders and seek improved productivity. Consequently, compromise and bargaining will be required. Encourage students to begin by stating their agreed objectives (to find savings of 10%) and to find issues on which they agree before going into detail on more problematic areas. As a general principle, suggest that they should only compromise where they get something in return – in other words, in conceding a point they should gain a concession in another area. This may involve looking at two or three points together – a common negotiating approach.

Follow-up

Set up a similar negotiation involving more participants, so that the negotiation involves teams.

20 Customer care

Introduction

This activity emphasizes the importance of looking after your customers – those who buy a product as well as those who buy a service.

Lead-in

In your introduction to this activity, ask about the distinction between internal customers (other employees within the same organization whom you serve) and external customers (those outside the company who pay you to provide them with a product or service). Ask students how far they serve internal as opposed to external customers in their work; and ask them whether they should be more focused on external customers.

Method

After the **B**s have administered the questionnaire to the **A**s, the partners can reverse roles.

Follow-up

1 The group can prioritize the different features of customer care listed in the questionnaire. One technique

for getting a large group to arrive at a final list is:

a) to get each pair to agree on a list of priorities; then

b) to get two pairs together to agree on a common list; then

c) to get two groups of four to agree on a common list, etc.

2 Get detailed feedback on how well your students feel their organizations serve their internal and their external customers, and how these two kinds of service could be improved.

21 Customer complaint

Introduction

This activity practises two important communication and business skills. **A**s have to turn an unhappy customer into a happy one. **B**s have to avoid being fobbed off with less than what they regard as their proper due.

Lead-in

Ask students:

- in what situations they have made complaints over the last few months
- whether their complaints have been well handled
- why it is important for companies to be able to deal efficiently with complaints.

Method

1 Allow adequate time for the heavier reading input or distribute the activity sheets before the session begins.

2 Ensure that both partners are clear about the final outcome of the discussion by getting them to write notes on the agreement reached and compare notes.

Follow-up

1 Get each pair to report back on their agreement and tabulate all the agreements on the board.

2 Get feedback on how the encounter between **B**s' firmness and **A**s' desire to win over the customer swayed the discussion one way or the other. Brainstorm language gambits which **A**s and **B**s might have used.

3 Get students to write **A**'s letter apologizing for the inconvenience, summarizing the agreement reached, etc.

22 Customs holdup

Introduction

This is a telephone conversation between two people with very different concerns.

Lead-in

To set up the theme, ask:

- what causes delays at frontiers
- what documents are needed
- how can delays be kept to a minimum
- if the problems at frontiers are the same everywhere
- if the solutions to the problems are the same everywhere.

Be tactful about the issue of corrupt officials – in some places mention of corruption may be acceptable only if it refers to other countries!

Method

Students have a reasonable amount of freedom in how to resolve the problem here. The discussion is led by **A** stating the problem and asking how it may be resolved. **B** responds and together the two positions are brought closer – or not, depending on the degree of obduracy held by the official, **B**, or rectitude held by **A**.

Follow-up

Some students might like to role play a face-to-face meeting at the frontier, with other students playing related roles, including the driver.

23 Employee morale

Introduction

This activity begins with an exchange of information, followed by discussion. It is important for the students to complete the first part satisfactorily before they start the second.

Lead-in

Ask the students in what way morale affects the way people work. What are the possible results of poor employee morale?

Method

1 Before the students begin, make it clear to **A**s and **B**s that they have different lists of suggestions for increasing company morale on their activity sheets. Underline the fact that they are not expected to compete by shortlisting more of their own key actions than their partners'. The objective is simply to get what they both agree is the best possible policy defined.

2 You could encourage them to simulate formal meetings with **B**s and then **A**s making short presentations of the ideas listed. They will need extra time to prepare this. This should then be followed by an open discussion of the merits of each idea in turn.

3 Students may wish to add their own ideas.

4 Ensure that each pair is clear about what it has agreed before calling a halt.

Follow-up
1 Brainstorm students' own additional ideas.
2 Discuss how far there is a group consensus and why some, if any, of the ideas are generally considered to be more feasible than others.
3 Get students to write a short report recommending a plan of action to the company's top management.

24 Entertaining visitors

Introduction
This is a fairly extensive telephone conversation in which two new business associates get to know each other a little and discuss possible entertainment for one of them, who is planning to visit the other.

Lead-in
Ask:
• what types of entertainment companies could provide for business associates in your country
• what sort of entertainment you would like if you were visiting other countries.

Method
• Much of the content here needs to be genuinely based on students' interests and preferences and on local entertainment available.
• An interesting way to do this is for **A** to explain to **B** what is available by referring to a local 'What's On' guide or newspaper.
• The conversation has three main parts after the initial introduction:
  i) outlining possible entertainment on offer
  ii) **B**'s preferences and interests
  iii) planning an entertainment itinerary for **B**'s visit.

Follow-up
• A fax from **A** confirming ideas and/or arrangements.
• Reversing roles: **B** should return the invitation and try to fix up entertainment that **A** would like.
• Repeat the activity placing emphasis on either very formal or very informal types of hospitality.

25 Environmentally friendly office

Introduction
This activity can be particularly interesting with groups of students from different companies, different sectors and different countries.

Lead-in
Ask students first of all what national laws exist on, for example, packaging, air and water pollution, etc. and ask if they know how legislation differs in any other country.

Method
Before the activity begins, you may wish to present or elicit some of the language which students may use in prioritizing the ideas, particularly comparative forms occurring in such expressions as: 'Oh no, I think using recycled paper is much more important than . . .'

Follow-up
1 Find out how many people feel this is a relevant and useful topic and how many do not think that safeguarding the environment is important.
2 Get feedback on students' own ideas. Additional suggestions might be:
  – turning off computers and other office equipment when not in use
  – avoiding unnecessary chemicals by, for example, using vegetable-based glues, pump-action containers rather than aerosols
  – using refillable laser printer cartridges
  – using scrap paper for notes rather than brand new memo pads
  – using electronic mail where possible rather than paper.
3 Questions for the group:
  – what environmentally friendly steps do you take in your own offices? What more could you and your colleagues do?
  – how environmentally conscious do you think your company is as a whole? What more could your company do?

26 Equal opportunities

Introduction
This is a straightforward collaborative discussion based on prioritizing a series of points.

Lead-in
Discuss the meaning of equal opportunities and the importance of the issue, with reference to students' own country/countries and/or experience.

Method
The objective of the activity is to prioritize a series of initiatives following discussion comparing the relative merits of different proposals. As each student has the same list of points, they should discuss the merits of each one, then decide on an order of importance.

Follow-up
- Learners can suggest initiatives which could be introduced in their own working environment to improve equal opportunities.
- Students can discuss what measures have already been taken and decide how effective they have been.

27 Franchising

Introduction
The activity is a face-to-face negotiation where both sides will need to compromise in order to reach an agreement.

Lead-in
Introduce the theme by asking students to name famous franchisors. Examples are McDonald's, Benetton, Hertz, Kentucky Fried Chicken. Ask:
- how franchises operate
- what is the relationship between franchisor and franchisee.

Method
Once students have read and understood their roles, **A**, the franchisee, should start by outlining some general objectives and by talking about the present situation. **B**, the franchisor, will need to be conciliatory. If the discussion follows the negotiating principle of 'only make a concession if you get something in return', then the result should be a lively exchange of offers and counter offers, but compromise will be necessary.

Follow-up
1 An exchange of letters outlining the basis for continued collaboration.
2 A jointly prepared statement explaining what they have agreed.

28 Health and safety

Introduction
The activity is based on a face-to-face discussion between colleagues, one more radical and more progressive than the other. Consequently, some persuasion will be required.

Lead-in
Discuss the issues involved in health and safety. How are these issues treated in the students' country/countries? How are they discussed and checked?

Method
1 **B** should start with a general outline of the health and safety position and some ideas on how to improve matters. **A** replies with comments on **B**'s remarks but proposes more radical changes.
2 Encourage students to paraphrase each other with expressions like 'So you think . . .' and 'What you're saying is . . .' before suggesting a slightly different emphasis.

Follow-up
A jointly-produced plan of action to present to other colleagues in the form of a short talk.

29 In-house magazine

Introduction
Discussing the contents of an in-house magazine gives the students an opportunity to discuss the type of information that should be included in such a magazine.

Lead-in
Ask:
- if their company has an in-house magazine
- if they read it
- how do they rate it
- how would they improve it.

Method
- There are really two parts to this activity. The full version involves drawing up a business plan for the magazine (see the section beginning: Identify the objectives of the magazine . . .) as well as deciding on the content. This version is likely to take up considerably more time.
- For students with less business experience or less time or both, the activity can centre on deciding on content alone.

Follow-up
After getting feedback on the various models of corporate communication proposed by students, widen the discussion to include other tools of internal communication:
- how do you make internal communication effective?
- how do you make internal communication two-way? etc.

30 Interview techniques

Introduction

The activity is a collaborative discussion, studying and sharing opinions before making an assessment.

Lead-in

Introduce the topic of interviewing by asking students about their experience of interviews and about what kind of questions they would expect to get in a job interview.

Method

Students sit side by side. There are three parts to the activity. First, students study the job advertisement, then classify the questions, then assess their usefulness in a job interview. In this last part they should jointly give a reason for their decision.

Follow-up

1 Use the questions as a framework for interviewing other students (or each other) for the job in question.
2 Study other job advertisements, work out likely questions for an interviewing panel, and set up interviews with other students.

31 Job application

Introduction

Although students may appreciate the fantasy element in the activity, they should nevertheless be encouraged to treat it as a serious exercise in recruitment. The respective partners should make initial assessments of the job or of the applicant, as appropriate.

Lead-in

Ask students:
- what types of job application forms they have filled in
- what the purpose of a form is
- whether a form is more effective than an open application.

Method

The procedure is as follows.
1 **B** (the applicant) calls **A** (the current PA who is leaving the job) to find out what has happened to his/her application.
2 **A** apologizes – has been very busy.
3 **B** asks **A** questions about the post while, alternately,
4 **A** asks **B** questions about his/her experience, languages, etc.
5 **A** should take the initiative to bring the call to an end, tell **B** what will happen next and say goodbye.

If appropriate telephones are not available, get pairs to sit back-to-back.

Follow-up

1 During the activity, monitor in particular the way the call starts and ends, and comment on the authenticity of these stages for the various pairs. Get good pairs to simulate model openings and closings for the others.
2 Discuss how the recruitment process might go on after this stage.
3 Get students to write a short letter from either the PA or the applicant, following on from this call.

32 Large versus small companies

Introduction

Large companies can be very powerful; small companies can be very flexible. So what are the advantages and disadvantages of each?

Lead-in

As a short lead-in, and before distributing the activity sheets, ask students whether they prefer working in a large or small organization. Elicit just one or two advantages and disadvantages for each.

Method

1 This exercise should be approached as a debate: **A** has to argue the advantages of working in a small company; **B** has to speak in favour of large organizations. Warn students that they may find themselves being asked to express opinions that they do not necessarily hold. Point out that this is good debating practice.
2 Roles can be reversed to see if further additional ideas are generated.

Follow-up

An **A** and a **B** from different pairs can be asked to debate again in front of the group.

33 Late payment of invoice

Introduction

This is a relatively short and simple activity, where two sides have conflicting interests. The topic relates to customer service: the creditor does not wish to upset a customer, but at the same time is keen to receive the money owed as soon as possible.

Lead-in
Ask:
- why late payment is a problem
- why do companies delay payment.

Method
1 **A**, the creditor, telephones **B**. Students should not sit face-to-face for telephoning tasks. If possible, use an internal phone line for a more effective role play.
2 **A** should secure a promise of when payment will be made.

Follow-up
Repeat the activity, reversing roles. See if the outcome is any different.

34 Management and leadership skills for women

Introduction
This activity is useful for training personnel as well as of general interest to women, in particular those in management or supervisory positions.

Lead-in
Ask students:
- if they think men and women have similar management skills
- if they think men and women have equal opportunities in the workplace in their country/countries.

Method
Although experienced trainers may be interested in spending the time necessary to devise training ideas for all five areas, most students will probably be happy to concentrate on discussing one problem area and devising a training idea for this area only. In this case pairs should:
1 discuss which area to concentrate on
2 discuss how best to handle the problem
3 devise a training idea.

Follow-up
1 Pairs give feedback to the group of the training ideas. If time permits, pairs can take over leadership of the group to try out the training idea they have devised.
2 Students who (rightly) point out that the problem areas are relevant to men just as much as to women, can be told that these areas were in fact identified for a successful real-life training programme aimed specifically at women. The legitimacy of identifying such areas can, of course, be debated.

35 Management qualities

Introduction
The activity is an informal face-to-face discussion which involves reading a list of points and prioritizing them.

Lead-in
As an introduction to the theme, ask students to brainstorm ideas on the qualities of a good manager and the attributes required in a management team.

Method
1 Students should first discuss the points listed and make sure they understand them all; then set about prioritizing them and come to a negotiated agreement on the right order.
2 If disagreements occur, compromise or trading of ideas may be necessary to reach an agreed order.

Follow-up
- Individual pairs can report reasons for their decisions and/or report any disagreements they had and how they were resolved.
- Some students may like to assess themselves on the basis of some of the qualities listed.

36 Market research

Introduction
The activity is a discussion between two people, one of whom has provided a service with which the other is not happy.

Lead-in
Introduce the theme by asking if students have any experience of market research and what they see as the advantages of market research for producers and service providers and for consumers. A possible answer is that the results of market research help producers to provide products or services which match consumer needs and wants.

Method
1 Preparation is vital. Monitor the preparation: it may be necessary, during the preparation, to prompt **A**, the hotelier, towards a set of demands to resolve the difficulty.
2 Once the discussion begins, **A** raises various objections to the survey technique and reporting. **B**, in assuring that the research is preliminary, avoids the issue and potentially fuels **A**'s dissatisfaction, since market research is very expensive.

3 The third stage should conclude the discussion, either with a resolution for how to proceed or with the relations breaking off in a somewhat hostile atmosphere.

Follow-up
Each side should write a letter to the other summarizing opinion and stating what should happen next.

37 Market survey

Introduction
This is a question and answer activity involving a questionnaire. It could be completed very quickly, though a variation could be that the respondent does not like some of the questions and challenges the design of the questionnaire!

Lead-in
Begin by prompting discussion on the purpose of market research and the importance of market surveys for companies.

Method
Simple questions and answers, with the interviewer noting the answers. **B** can give genuine responses.

A variation could be that **B** plays a role where the respondent really likes to talk a great deal around the questions, so delaying the (impatient) interviewer.

Follow-up
Reverse the roles and repeat the activity. Get students to repeat the activity several times with other students or teachers, in order to collect data for a group of people. Students could also design their own questionnaire on a different topic of their choosing.

38 Meeting arrangements

Introduction
The activity involves a telephone call and making arrangements to meet but each individual has a different attitude. **B** (the agent) is fairly reluctant to devote time to **A**'s products – or a meeting. The objective is to agree on a meeting.

Lead-in
Discuss the role of agents and the nature of the manufacturer–agent relationship. When is the relationship problematic? One possible answer is when the agent is not effective or when he/she has other priorities or sells competing products.

Method
1 As with other telephoning activities, use an internal line, or seat students back-to-back. They should have a pencil to take notes.
2 Remind students that good telephoning technique includes summarizing any agreement at the end of the call to confirm that everything is clear.
3 Give feedback and repeat the exercise if necessary, specifically to improve telephoning technique.

Follow-up
1 Write a fax confirming details of the arrangement.
2 Reverse the roles and repeat the exercise, or set up a similar situation perhaps based on students' actual commitments.

39 Mission statement

Introduction
This is a potentially difficult and time-consuming activity which requires the exercise of a variety of different skills, including note-taking and writing. Students' efforts will, however, be rewarded in having given thought to some fundamental questions about the nature and *raison d'être* of their own business organization. Have available some mission statements from real companies to show to students either at the activity or at the feedback stage.

Lead-in
Ask students:
• if their company has a mission statement
• and, if so, what it is
• what its purpose is
• if it is useful.

Method
1 Before starting, discuss with the group the kind of language in general and the typical structures associated with mission statements. Write suggestions on the board for reference during the exercise, for example: we want to . . ., we need . . ., we believe in . . ., we believe that . . .
2 Students in pairs will move from discussion, through note-taking, to drafting and redrafting their own statements. Give as much help as possible. If available, provide students with word processing facilities while working towards the final draft.

Follow-up
1 Ask pairs to read out their own drafts. Look for common threads to develop in the discussion phase.

Teachers' notes

2 Ask students:
- what mission statements achieve
- who should write them
- how much the personnel of the company as a whole should be consulted during the drafting stages.

40 Pay versus benefits

Introduction
This activity can be of general interest to all managers and of specific professional interest to managers involved in human resources and personnel.

Lead-in
Ask students how companies that they know remunerate their employees.

Method
Present the activity in general terms and go through the details of the current package with the group to ensure the terms are clear, before handing out the activity sheets. Notes:
- PRB. The manager earned a performance-related bonus of £10,650 out of a possible maximum of £20,000 last year.
- Long-term disability cover. This is a form of insurance which provides the manager with an income in the event of his/her being unable to work for an extended period through accident or illness. (The cover is private because the government of the country in which both the students work does not make adequate provision for this.)
- Parking. The company currently pays for the manager to park in a city centre car park every day when he/she comes to work. The company does not have its own car park and cheap parking is impossible to find.
- Annual health screening. A detailed medical examination.

Follow-up
1 Get feedback on the results of each negotiation. Clearly, a figure close to £40,000 is good for **A** (the personnel manager) while **B** will have aimed to get more. Find out how close to the total of £40,000 each pair were.
2 Ask whether the fact that the manager (**B**) only managed to earn just over 50% of his potential PRB last year reflects well or badly on him/her. Can we draw any conclusions about his/her quality as a manager?

3 Ask how many of the group have experience of performance-related pay and how they feel about it.

41 Performance appraisal

Introduction
The activity is an internal discussion meeting, therefore informal, leading to a decision on a problematic employee.

Lead-in
Discuss the meaning of performance appraisal and ask:
- what its purpose is
- if performance appraisal is used in the students' country.

Method
B should start by introducing the purpose of the discussion and outlining the problem. The discussion should move from general observations and opinions to specific decisions and agreement.

Follow-up
- Joint preparation of a memo outlining the agreement reached.
- There is also scope for general class discussion of the issues involved in problems such as those outlined in the activity.

42 Presenting information

Introduction
The activity is an opportunity to present information in a well-structured manner and to respond to questions. See also Activity 14 on Company presentation.

Lead-in
To introduce the theme, ask students to brainstorm the most important characteristics of good presentation technique. Possible answers include: well prepared, well organized, appropriate and relevant, clear, enthusiastically presented and supported by good visuals.

Method
Two minutes is very little preparation time and three minutes is a very short talk. Offer a model as an example. The key objective is to get over a limited amount of information in a well structured and coherent fashion, with an introduction, a middle and an end. After each presentation, the partner and other students (and you) can ask questions.

Follow-up
- Allow longer preparation time for slightly longer talks.
- Allow students to choose other topics, which may be business or study related, or concern personal interests.
- Allow extra preparation time for the inclusion of a visual support.

43 Press and public relations

Introduction
The activity is a potentially highly conflictive interview. **A** has to be very calm under pressure from both the situation and from aggressive questioning by the press.

Lead-in
Discuss the importance of public relations and the relationship between PR and corporate image (see introduction in activity section).

Method
A face-to-face interview. It would be fun to video record this if possible, and play it back as part of a news extract or documentary on pollution.

Follow-up
Extend the video idea to build the interview into a discussion of the problem of industrial pollution. A further possibility would be to bring in other roles, such as environmental campaigners, employees, relatives of employees, other managers, local residents, etc., and have a wider debate in the shape of a public meeting.

44 Product endorsement

Introduction
Michael Jackson and Pepsi became a famous double act. But who benefited in the end?

Lead-in
Lead in by asking for examples of product endorsements by famous people and discussing briefly the advantages and disadvantages of this form of product promotion.

Method
This activity is essentially a preliminary negotiation involving an information gap. Students should prepare a strategy before they begin the negotiation and should try to anticipate the arguments of the other side as part of their preparation.

Follow-up
1 Get feedback from each pair on the development and outcome of each negotiation.
2 Discuss the advantages and disadvantages of product endorsement in more detail. If necessary, point out that sometimes the arrangement can backfire, for example if the pop star endorsing your product is accused of child abuse or the athlete endorsing your running shoes consistently fails to win races.

45 Production delays

Introduction
This is a telephone activity based on serious organization problems in a subsidiary.

Lead-in
Ask:
- what the relationship is between a head office and a subsidiary
- when problems arise
- how problems can be resolved.

Method
A, at the head office, telephones the subsidiary to know what is going on. **A** may choose to insist on visiting the subsidiary. As usual with telephone activities, prompt students to summarize any agreement at the end.

Follow-up
- **A** should write a confirmatory fax, outlining main points of the discussion.
- **B** should write a memo to an English-speaking colleague in Portugal.
- The situation could be extended to a face-to-face meeting.

46 Profit and loss account

Introduction
The activity is basically a telephoned information transfer between colleagues, though explanations are required to support the details.

Lead-in
As a lead-in to the subject, check that students understand what a profit and loss account is. Ask them to say if the following statements are true (T) or false (F):
- it shows the health of a company at a given moment (F)
- it shows the trading performance of a company in a particular time period (T)

- it shows the principal costs a company has to meet (T)
- it shows forecast sales for the coming year. (F)

Method

1 **B** asks a series of questions to complete information required on the latest profit and loss account for a sister company. He/she also asks a series of questions in order to clarify certain aspects.
2 **B** should paraphrase or repeat certain answers to make sure there are no mistakes in the transfer of the information or in understanding the answers to the further questions.

Follow-up

Find other examples of profit and loss accounts and assess the strength of companies' trading positions.

---

47 Project management

Introduction

The activity is based on an informal face-to-face meeting between a project leader and his/her assistant. There is a strong disagreement, so diplomacy and tact are important qualities for both sides.

Lead-in

Discuss the purpose of project planning and its importance in industry.

Method

In group meetings an assistant would be unlikely to criticize his or her boss's plans. Remind students that in this case, the meeting is private and informal and the disagreements are real. They must, however, reach agreement. This discussion may be lengthy, since there are several points to raise and to agree on.

Follow-up

Together they may prepare a joint plan to present to other members of the team.

---

48 Quality

Introduction

Increasingly, companies compete on quality, but quality cannot be achieved without the involvement of the whole workforce. So a good quality programme will involve people – often people who were previously sceptical about such programmes.

Lead-in

What does quality mean? What effect does poor quality have on customers? How important is quality for competing in the market place?

Method

Getting each pair to choose the six most desirable features for their quality programme may require a generous time allowance. Start by getting each pair to eliminate the features that neither member wants to retain.

Follow-up

1 Compare the shortlists drawn up by the different pairs. How similar are they?
2 Discuss how such quality programmes can be implemented.
3 Ask students what experience they have had of quality assurance programmes both as employees and as consumers (noticing a conspicuous improvement in a company's products or services).

---

49 Quiz 1

Introduction

This activity can last as long or as short a time as you want, so make a clear decision in advance on the time limit you want to set and whether you are going to introduce it as a quick end-of-lesson quiz lasting ten minutes or a main activity involving lots of discussion and supplementary questioning.

Method

- As can ask **B**s all the questions and then reverse roles. This can also be good listening practice if **B**s are not shown the sheet.
- **A**s and **B**s can ask each other questions in turn.
- **A**s can ask **B**s the questions in Quiz 1 and then **B**s can ask **A**s the questions in Quiz 2.

Follow-up

Lots of possibilities for discussion and a real opportunity for members of a group to learn more about each other and to get to know each other better.

---

50 Quiz 2

See Quiz 1

51 Raising finance

Introduction

The activity is based on a friendly meeting between a company executive and an independent financial adviser.

Lead-in

To introduce the topic, discuss raising finance, ensuring that students understand the various ways a company may choose to do this as explained in the students' introductions.

Method

1 Thorough preparation is important: students need to understand the balance sheet.
2 **A**, representing the company, outlines the present position of the company. He/she wants advice on the likelihood of raising finance.
3 **B** responds by asking for more information and then answers, giving reasons for his/her opinions.
4 Encourage students to check their understanding of what the other says by paraphrasing. Elicit/suggest phrases like 'So, you're saying . . .' and 'So what you mean is . . .'

Follow-up

Look at examples of balance sheets from company reports. Identify the key figures to assess the health or otherwise of the companies involved.

52 Recruitment

Introduction

This activity involves finding the most suitable candidate for the job.

Lead-in

- Discuss recruitment procedures experienced by your students, either as job applicants or as employment providers.
- Give some practice in paraphrasing information so that students do not read out the file cards verbatim.

Method

Judge whether students are able to structure the telephone meeting without help or whether you should advise them to postpone discussion until all the candidates have been described. Encourage genuine summarizing and paraphrasing rather than reading out the file cards verbatim. Give an example of how to do it.

Follow-up

1 Get feedback from all the pairs on which applicant was preferred and why.
2 Discuss the advantages and disadvantages of different stages in the conventional recruitment process:
   - are references reliable? Is testing reliable?
   - can a potential employer really learn anything from an interview?
   - how well do interviewers interview?

53 Recycling

Introduction

The activity involves an informal face-to-face discussion between colleagues. The essential objective is to agree on priorities and on a plan of action.

Lead-in

Discuss recycling, its purpose and value and students' experience of it.

Method

The activity has two parts. Students should decide on the three key advantages of recycling and any drawbacks involved. They should then formulate a policy for the company involved.

Follow-up

- Combine this activity with other environment-related studies from other sources. (Activity 43 also concerns an environmental issue.)
- Students may also comment on recycling policies in companies or institutions they are familiar with, as well as domestic recycling.
- Design a questionnaire to find out the extent of recycling and people's views on the subject.

54 Relocation

Introduction

This is a difficult activity because the positions of the two parties are initially quite far apart. You should monitor the process by which the students succeed in finding – or fail to find – a solution to a problem which has no obvious solution.

Lead-in

Briefly discuss the notions of win–win, win–lose and lose–lose in negotiation and ask the students to describe business situations in which it is better not to compromise.

Method

Be prepared for the activity to last only a short time (in the case of neither party being willing to compromise) or quite a long time (where there is readiness to compromise). If some pairs finish the activity quickly, get them to write each other follow-up letters.

Follow-up

1 Get feedback on the outcomes for the different pairs in the group and the process by which the outcomes were arrived at.
2 Ask students if they have ever been involved in negotiating a problem where the two sides were so far apart that there seemed little chance of agreement. Discuss different strategies in such a situation.
3 Get students to write formal letters to each other as **A** or **B** with their versions of the decisions reached.

---

55 Sales targets

Introduction

This activity is a straightforward exchange of figures between the two partners. It may therefore last rather less time than a first glance suggests. Pocket calculators will be useful.

Lead-in

Ask:
- why setting targets is important
- what happens if targets are not met.

Method

There are two sets of figures to exchange:
- each partner has a couple of figures missing for the other regions
- each partner has only his/her own revised figures, so the procedure might be:
  a) exchange the missing fourth quarter figures for the other regions
  b) calculate and agree on the totals for the other regions
  c) calculate own revised total (strictly speaking it is not necessary to exchange all the revised figures unless each wants to check the other's figures in detail)
  d) add the two revised totals and compare with the other regional totals
- as you can see from the figures below, your students have indeed won the prize – but don't give the game away: let them find out for themselves.

Follow-up

1 Reproduce the table on the board and get students to fill in the missing figures.
2 Discuss figures central to the students' own work.
3 Discuss this kind – and other kinds – of incentive for sales people and others.

Figures in $US	North	West	South	East
First quarter	93,137	94,005	85,211	93,140
Second quarter	101,104	98,276	85,439	99,505
Third quarter	103,721	99,422	87,624	102,099
Fourth quarter	95,106	100,471	89,423	102,600
Total	**393,068**	**392,174**	**347,697**	**397,344**

Figures in $US	West Central Initial	West Central Revised	East Central Initial	East Central Revised	Central Revised Total
First quarter	46,010	46,910	47,194	47,668	94,578
Second quarter	48,763	48,963	51,309	51,309	100,272
Third quarter	49,345	49,727	51,499	51,699	101,426
Fourth quarter	49,557	50,847	51,446	50,230	101,077
Total	**193,675**	**196,447**	**201,448**	**200,906**	**397,353**

---

56 Small talk 1

Introduction

This is difficult but the activity practises a very important skill – steering the conversation. Each box contains:
- four nouns
- three verbs
- three adjectives

Method

Ten minutes for the activity. Compare scores and experiences at the end: which were the easiest and which were the most difficult words to elicit and why? Then reverse the roles.

Follow-up

1 Discuss the importance of taking the initiative and steering the conversation.

2 Ask selected pairs to perform in front of the others.
3 Get feedback from the group on successful and less successful steering gambits.

57 Small talk 2

Introduction
Tell your students that they have the opportunity to temporarily assume a new persona. Encourage them to invent interesting ones.

Lead-in
- Lead in with brainstorming on ways of opening a conversation in a plane.
- Encourage students to use realistic gambits to open.
- Talk about balance between the two members: you do not want to hear one talking a lot more than the other. You expect to hear lots of questions from both partners.

Method
1 Students fill in the form.
2 Students talk to each other for ten minutes.

Follow-up
Get feedback from all members of the group, for example:
- what was the most interesting thing you heard?
- what was the most surprising thing you heard?
- what future do you predict for the person you met?

58 Spare parts

Introduction
The activity is a telephone dialogue, based on information transfer. Both sides have information that they need to convey. As purchaser and supplier they need to reach agreement on an urgent order.

Lead-in
Discuss:
- the relationship between purchaser and supplier
- the importance of spare parts for certain types of equipment.

Method
Same procedure as in other telephone activities. Both sides need to refer to the information they have, citing needs and production schedules respectively. The conversation will realistically include pauses while the supplier checks information and the purchaser considers what he/she is told. Stalling language, space filling and supporting silence is important in telephoning. In

feedback, suggest improvements – thinking in particular about these aspects of language.

Follow-up
A fax confirming the order from both sides.

59 Team building

Introduction
We used to have leaders; now we have teams. Success depends more and more on picking and developing a winning team.

Lead-in
This exercise is designed to help students understand that colleagues may work in very different ways, yet each may make a vital contribution to meeting shared objectives. Ask students about their experiences of working together with people who have a different approach from their own.

Method
1 Students may wish to define what kind of project it is that they are working on. This in turn will influence what kind of people they need to carry it through. Parameters for the project could include:
- objective
- time scale
- budget
- overall size of team
- functions of key team members.
2 Students can discuss:
- the functions (jobs) needed for the project as a whole
- the roles they themselves will play
- the roles to be played by two or more other people to be recruited to the team.

Follow-up
1 Find out where students feel they might be on the wheel and what kind of person they feel is required for the job they currently do.
2 Discuss whether the wheel could be a useful tool in creating balanced teams.
3 Get students to write a job advertisement for one of the missing team members, describing the characteristics of the person they are looking for.

60 Time management

Introduction
Everybody in employment will have an opinion on this issue. The fairly simple matching exercise is intended

as a preliminary to discussion within each pair of more detailed and additional ways of managing one's time more successfully.

Lead-in

Ask students about the importance of:

• deadlines
• schedules
• keeping appointments
• time-management systems e.g. filofaxes.

Method

1 **A** presents problem 1 to **B**. **B** chooses the most appropriate solution from the four alternatives – a, b, c and d – and proposes this to **A**. Note that both the list of problems and the list of solutions for **A** and **B** are different.

2 **A** continues with problems 2, 3 and 4 with **B** suggesting the best remaining solution each time. If **B** has chosen wrongly, it will finally become apparent. **A** and **B** can now sort out any mistakes in selection together.

3 Roles are now reversed and **B** presents a new problem 1 to **A**, etc.

Follow-up

1 Elicit the time management problems that students have and the solutions that they recommend to each other.

2 Get the group as a whole to formulate some golden rules for time management. These might be along the lines of:

– do it now
– get rid of clutter
– plan your day.

61 Training priorities

Introduction

This is a short activity based on working together to study a list of options and to agree on their relative values.

Lead-in

Ask learners what kind of training they think is most useful for companies working in international business. They should draw up a list of options which could then be compared with the training types presented in this activity.

Method

1 To prepare for the activity, both students should fully understand the information on the company involved.

2 Then there are two stages: first to prioritize the nine different training options, then to eliminate the least useful. They may also decide that others could be postponed until later.

Follow-up

Prepare a short presentation to the board of directors, outlining key training needs, requesting full financial resources, time and full backing from the training department. The presentation should explain why the training is so important.

62 Transportation

Introduction

Quite a challenging role play, involving a sales pitch from one side and an important comparison of two offers followed by a decision from the prospective purchaser.

Lead-in

Ask:

• what types of transport are used for what types of goods?
• what problems face transportation companies?
• what problems face companies using transportation services?

Method

The activity requires a good level of preparation and understanding of their roles from both sides. Essentially **A** has to listen to **B** trying to sell a particular transportation service and at the same time compare it with an offer already on the table from a Greek company. **A**'s role is the more complicated one, and he/she is also the decision maker. When ready, **B** calls with a prepared sales pitch.

Follow-up

Both sides can write a letter confirming their requirements (**A**) or their offer (**B**).

63 Work environment

Introduction

The activity is a face-to-face discussion, involving a sharing of both information and opinions. The atmosphere should be constructive and positive.

Lead-in

Introduce the theme by talking about good and bad working conditions and their consequences for productivity, morale, staff turnover and sickness.

Method

1 **A** begins by outlining general intentions and reminding the employees' representative of the company's concerns, while also not wanting to raise expectations too high. Note the low budget available.
2 The objective is to reach a satisfactory position, where both sides feel they have achieved something.
3 Students should note what they agree and summarize it.

Follow-up

- **A** can write a glowing account of improvements being made, either for company notice boards or for an in-house magazine.
- **B** can write a letter supporting the improvements but pointing out other areas where progress should be made and requesting a longer term commitment to these further improvements.

64 Work rotas

Introduction

A fairly straightforward conflict in this face-to-face informal meeting over holiday plans and production schedules. There might just be room for compromise, or else **B** will simply refuse – but must explain why and get **A** to understand the position.

Lead-in

Introduce the theme by asking about potential conflict of interest over holiday plans and company requirements. Family holidays and school holidays may coincide with companies' busiest times. How can such difficulties be resolved?

Method

A, the boss, has a meeting with **B**, a line supervisor, to see if he/she can change holiday plans. **A** should explain why and offer some compensation or alternative deal. **B** may simply refuse or enter into some kind of negotiation. Of course, a further problem will be to present the family with the changed holiday arrangements, which might be disastrous.

Follow-up

- Discuss the responsibility of a manager to think of employees' general well-being, including family circumstances. Ask what would happen if the company decided to pay the holiday cancellation fee and to insist on the supervisor changing plans.
- Discuss the extent to which company needs prevail over personal or family needs in a given culture.

65 Works council

Introduction

A fantasy activity for general discussion for all categories of business personnel. Tell students that they can choose more than one option but that they must decide clearly how all the money is to be spent.

Lead-in

Ask students about joint decision making in their companies. Ask if there is a works council and in what areas there is consultation between employer and employees.

Method

Open discussion within each pair.

Follow-up

1 Get feedback from the group. Alternatively use the method described in the Teachers' notes to Activity 20, *Follow-up 1*, to get the whole group to reach a collective decision.
2 Get feedback on students' own ideas. Which of the ideas given did they think were best and which were worst?
3 Get students to write to the rest of the staff on behalf of the works council, explaining how the money is to be spent and giving reasons.

Student A

Material for photocopying

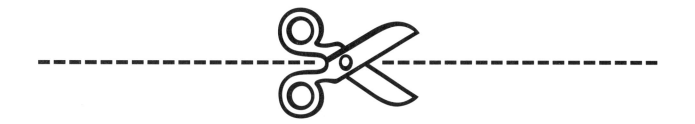

(Introducing self and others; questioning)

Ice breakers are short activities which help people get to know each other at the beginning of a training course.

Get the following information about your partner. One of you can ask all the questions first or you can take it in turns to ask each question.

---

1 Professional

Find out your partner's:

- name
- company
- company's activity (in one sentence)
- job title
- department
- job responsibilities (in one sentence)
- office location.

---

2 Personal

Find out about your partner's:

- home
- family
- education
- favourite sport
- tastes in music
- languages.

YOU START.

(Measuring and calculating; negotiating; urging)

Advertising is one aspect of promotional activity used by companies to increase consumer awareness of the company and its products, and to improve sales performance.

You work in the marketing department of a sports shoe manufacturer. You have contacted an advertising agency and asked for suggestions for a campaign to promote your brand, Sporto. You want to run a campaign within a budget of £250,000 – no more.

YOU:

- sponsored the local football team last year but the team performed badly and received very little national television coverage
- think the football team will do well this year – they have a rich chairman, five new players and a new manager
- want the brand name Sporto to be promoted nationally
- have little interest in a specifically local market
- think international recognition would be a good bonus
- want some guarantee in terms of increased sales
- want to be involved in planning the details of any advertising campaign
- think TV advertising is too expensive.

YOU START.

© Penguin Books 1996

3   AGENDAS

(Agreeing/disagreeing; judging)

An agenda consists of the points that will be discussed in a meeting, in order to reach agreed objectives. Not all meetings have written agendas, but everyone should understand the objectives of a meeting and know what issues will be discussed, within an agreed time.

As project leader for a new quality programme, you have sent the following agenda to various colleagues and have asked for comments. One of them telephones you to discuss the planned agenda.

Departmental Quality Development Group

Agenda for Meeting

Time: 9.30 – 11.00
Date: January 14, 19—.
Place: Head Office, Room 2–17.

1. Customer feedback
2. Internal suggestions
3. Quality standards

Comments welcome – Please call

YOU:

- **have recently been abroad and have not had time to prepare a full agenda – you specifically welcome suggestions on improving this one**

- **think quality improvement is the key element for business success**

- **are working hard to create a total quality ethos in the company**

- **welcome ideas on quality but you are sure that a separate publication or newsletter is not necessary.**

YOUR PARTNER WILL START.

© Penguin Books 1996

(Measuring and calculating; correcting; obliging; regretting)

Bank charges are the fees paid to banks for the various services they provide. Banks charge interest on the money they lend, but also charge fees for setting up loans and overdrafts, or for assisting in funds, transfers, currency exchange, the provision of references, advice and a wide range of financial services.

Your bank has sent you the following notification of a funds transfer from a Chinese customer. You notice that you have been credited with only £1,995 when it should have been £2,020 less a £10 handling charge. You call the bank.

CREDIT BANK INTERNATIONAL

King's Cross   Branch   Date: *24 June 19——.*

Please note that we have credited your account.

Your ref.   *Lee Pen & Co – China*

Invoice dated   *2 May 19——.*   Invoice total   *£2,020.00*

To   *F. Petersson S.A.*   Account number: *00878654*

AMOUNT   *£1,995.00p*

For Credit Bank International
HLT

YOU START.

© Penguin Books 1996

5 BUDGET PRESENTATION

(Questioning; judging; hesitating; forecasting)

Budgeting involves combining sales forecasts with expected costs. Effective planning requires accurate budgeting and also a clear understanding of the effects of variations in any particular figure, from raw material costs to unit price or promotional costs.

At a finance meeting you have to present the following sales budget for an existing product, a mobile telephone called the CX20.

Invite interruptions and questions. If you cannot give all the information that you are asked for, promise to provide that information at a future meeting.

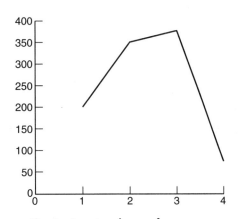

Fig. 1 Forecast sales over four quarters

| One: 200 | Two: 350 | Three: 375 | Four: 75 | Total = 1,000 |

Fig. 2 Unit sales forecast over four quarters

Estimated effect of 10% unit price increase

Unit price:	£150	£165
Sales:	£150,000	£160,875
Total cost of sales:	£50,000	£50,000
Cost of selling:	£78,000	£78,000
Total costs:	£128,000	£128,000
Gross profit:	**£22,000**	**£32,875**

Estimated effect of 10% unit price increase would be a 2.5% drop in sales.

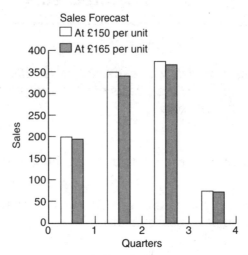

Fig. 3   Estimated effect of 10% unit price increase

| One: 195 | Two: 341 | Three: 367 | Four: 72 | Total = 975 |

Note:

The cost of selling covers all promotional activity, including advertising, sales commissions, fees to agents and distributors, distribution, and storage and transport. The cost of sales includes fixed overheads (rent, heating, wages and salaries) and variable costs (raw materials, overtime payments).

YOU:

- think market share is not going to be greatly affected by a small price increase
- have cut costs but cannot do so any more
- think the market is rather price sensitive and that sales will fall, but that a temporary loss in sales will not be significant in the long term
- feel that improved profits now will help to boost sales in the future
- do not think competitors will lower their prices.

YOU START.

          © Penguin Books 1996

(Telling; sequencing; emphasizing)

An anecdote is a short story which you tell, usually about something which happened to you or to someone you know. Being able to tell a story is a very useful skill, both generally and in business: when talking to the person sitting next to you during a plane journey, for example. This activity gives you the chance to practise telling a story in a business context.

You and your partner are going to tell each other a story about a company. You will begin the story using the first sentence below, then your partner will take over, then you will take over again, and so on. Try to talk for about one and a half minutes each time before handing over.

> 1 When Jo Batsoukis and Les Chan left business school, they immediately founded a company making . . .

> 3 But they were beginning to have financial problems. . . .

> 5 Then one morning came a telephone call from the President of . . .

YOU START.

7   BUSINESS ETIQUETTE

(Agreeing/disagreeing; questioning)

Business etiquette – forms of polite behaviour – can vary not just from one country to another, but also from one profession to another, from company to company, even from department to department. This exercise will help you measure how far you and your partner follow different codes of etiquette.

Five areas of business etiquette are listed below. In each case, tell your partner what the rules or conventions are in the company where you work, using the questions to help you. Then get your partner to tell you how his or her conventions differ from yours and discuss the differences.

---

1 **Shaking hands:** do you shake hands with people:
- when you first meet them?
- every time you meet them?
- when you haven't seen them for a long time?
- when you say goodbye to them?
- never?

Are the rules different for men and for women?

---

2 **Names:** do you:
- call people you know by their first name or by their family name (using Mr, Mrs, Miss or Ms)?
- call people you have just met by their first name or by their family name (using Mr, Mrs, Miss or Ms)?

---

3 **Men's dress:**
- what do men wear to work?
- are there any rules telling men what they must wear?
- do men always have to wear a tie?
- does what they wear change according to the weather?
- would it be possible for men to wear shorts in very hot weather?

---

4 **Women's dress:**
- what do women wear to work?
- are there any rules telling women what they must wear?
- are women free to wear any jewellery they like?
- do women always have to wear stockings or tights?
- does what they wear change according to the weather?

---

5 **Compliments:**
- do female work colleagues compliment each other on their dress or general appearance?
- do male work colleagues compliment each other on their dress or general appearance?
- do female work colleagues compliment male colleagues on their dress or general appearance?

Now your partner will ask you about five other areas of business etiquette.

YOU START.

   © Penguin Books 1996

8 BUSINESS GIFTS

Student A

(Agreeing/disagreeing; emphasizing; permitting; vetoing)

Business gifts are sometimes sent to customers or clients in the hope that they build goodwill – and help secure business. In many cases the activity is perfectly reasonable and open – but in some cases the practice of offering and receiving gifts is connected to dubious behaviour, malpractice or illegal activities.

You are one of two purchasing directors in a large manufacturing company with a $70m turnover. One of your purchasers has been sent a case of Grand Cru Bordeaux wine by a supplier. Some of your management colleagues feel he should not have accepted this gift. At present the company has no policy on receiving gifts.

Together with your partner, decide on a new company policy on receiving gifts.

Prior to your meeting you draw up the following options:

MEMO

To:
From:
Date:

Gifts – what to do??
– No gifts should be accepted.
– Only gifts up to a certain agreed value should be accepted.
– All gifts should be pooled and used as prizes in the company Christmas raffle.

YOU:

- **tend to think that gifts compromise your colleagues – they are more likely to buy from companies who supply the best gifts, not those offering the best products and the best service.**

YOUR PARTNER WILL START.

© Penguin Books 1996

33

(Knowing; correcting)

When reading the press in a foreign language, understanding the initials can sometimes create almost as many problems as understanding the words.

Here is a quiz to test and increase your knowledge of some basic – and not so basic – sets of initials which you could meet when reading the business press in English. First test your partner on what the following sets of initials stand for. Then your partner will give you a similar test. Then compare scores. Warning: each test gets harder as you go along!

1	**MD**	(Managing Director)
2	**VP**	(Vice-President)
3	**R&D**	(Research and Development)
4	**PA**	(Personal Assistant/Per Annum)
5	**MBA**	(Master in Business Administration)
6	**EU**	(European Union)
7	**GATT**	(General Agreement on Tariffs and Trade)
8	**IBM**	(International Business Machines)
9	**SAS**	(Scandinavian Airline Systems)
10	**WP**	(Word processor or word processing)
11	**RAM**	(Random Access Memory)
12	**AGM**	(Annual General Meeting)
13	**GNP**	(Gross National Product)
14	**VAT**	(Value Added Tax)
15	**The 4 Ps**	(Price, Promotion, Packaging, Place)
16	**ILO**	(International Labour Organization)

YOUR PARTNER WILL START.

© Penguin Books 1996

Buying and selling a product or service, especially abroad, often involves negotiation – an agreement through discussion of the terms of the buying and selling arrangement.

You are an import-export agent specializing in high-tech consumer products. You want to negotiate an agreement with the foreign manufacturer of an exciting new computer game. You are now going to have a meeting with this person (your partner). Using the table below, negotiate an agreement covering:

- **the number of units that you will agree to take: although you think it's a good product, you are careful about committing yourself too much to a small, unknown company**
- **the terms of payment**
- **your discount on the standard price.**

Quantity	Terms	Discount
10,000 *Score: 25 points*	90 days *Score: 25 points*	30% *Score: 25 points*
20,000 *Score: 20 points*	60 days *Score: 20 points*	20% *Score: 20 points*
30,000 *Score: 15 points*	30 days *Score: 15 points*	15% *Score: 15 points*
40,000 *Score: 10 points*	Half in advance Half within 30 days *Score: 10 points*	10% *Score: 10 points*
50,000 *Score: 5 points*	In advance *Score: 5 points*	5% *Score: 5 points*

YOU would also like the manufacturer to provide:

- **a CD-Rom version of the software as soon as possible. There is huge demand for CD-Rom-based games in your country. Score 5 points for delivery of a CD-Rom version in 6 months, 10 points for delivery in 4 months, 15 points for delivery in 2 months**

- **new packaging adapted to the local market: score 5 points if the manufacturer agrees**

- **promotional literature in the main language of your region: score 5 points if the manufacturer agrees.**

Negotiate an agreement with the manufacturer. Aim to get as many points as possible but do not reveal your scoring system to your partner. At the end of the negotiation, summarize your agreement under all six headings (quantity, terms, discount, adaptation, packaging and literature) and compare your score with your partner's. Remember: your objective is to get as many points as possible but also to carry on doing business with the manufacturer after the negotiation is finished.

YOUR PARTNER WILL START.

© Penguin Books 1996

(Forecasting; judging; urging; negotiating)

Cashflow problems occur when a company has insufficient funds available to meet existing operating costs. A company may have full order books, but still suffer from funding problems while they wait for customers to pay.

You work in the finance department of a company which has received an urgent order for 150 trailers from the government of a Gulf state. The trailers must be custom-built to meet highly specific requirements and must be delivered in only three months.

Your existing production budget is not able to meet this order on top of present cost commitments. To raise the necessary funds would involve a 25% increase in expenditure to buy the materials and to hire workers and a further £200,000 in other costs, making a total increase of £550,000. This is well above the estimated closing cash balance for the year.

You have a meeting with a colleague in the marketing department to discuss the order. You have to decide what to do. Here is a copy of the cash budget for the present year:

Opening cash balance (£)	220,500
Add receipts	
Collections from customers	
(Sales less £180,000 increase in debtors)	2,400,000
Total cash available	2,620,500
Less payments	
For materials	
(Purchases less £80,000 increase in creditors)	400,000
For selling expenses	380,000
For direct labour	600,000
Manufacturing overheads	500,000
For capital equipment	250,000
For general expenses	92,000
Total cash needed	2,222,000
Closing cash balance	398,500

YOU:

- **think that the £550,000 required to meet the order cannot be raised within the existing cash budget**
- **need to know the time schedule for payment**
- **would want the following terms: 25% payment with order + 25% on delivery + the balance within three months, i.e. payment completed within six months**
- **usually schedule payments for your products over twelve months from the order. This would be unacceptable**
- **wonder if other sources of finance could help you to meet this order.**

YOUR PARTNER WILL START.

    © Penguin Books 1996

12 COMPANY OF THE YEAR Student A

(Agreeing/disagreeing; emphasizing; judging; urging)

One way of encouraging small businesses to grow is to organize competitions with prizes for young companies with special entrepreneurial flair. A money prize can be very useful for a company with ambitions to expand but limited finance to do so. The only danger for competitors, successful and unsuccessful, is for them to spend more time on the competition than on doing business!

You and your partner together run a successful small business. You have just won a regional young business competition sponsored by the local press, television, local government and the local chamber of commerce.

First decide on the following:

Company activity: . . . .

Main markets: . . . .

Turnover: . . . .

Net profit margin: . . . .

Number of employees: . . . .

Now decide how you are going to spend the £100,000 first prize. Some suggestions are given below. Share your ideas with your partner and agree on a common plan. You should decide which options to go for and how much of the money to spend on each. Draw up a final investment plan for the whole sum of money.

YOU would like to:

- **organize a well-earned and much needed holiday for both managing partners**

- **lease new offices (since you feel that your existing offices are not very good for your image)**

- **save (some of) it**

- **upgrade the company's computer system**

- **buy a market survey from an agency to research new markets**

- **commission a management consultancy to do a full audit of your company's finances and management procedures**

- **buy management training for you and your partner so that you are both ready for the next step in your company's growth.**

List your own ideas.

YOU START.

(Declining/rejecting; judging; liking and preferring)

Company organization is sometimes described in an organization chart or organigram, often a simplified diagram showing areas of responsibility for key personnel.

Your company, Altman Kopp, is involved in negotiations with a competitor, KEP Ltd, over a possible merger. In an informal meeting, you discuss ways to combine the two businesses into a single organization, allowing for the following facts:

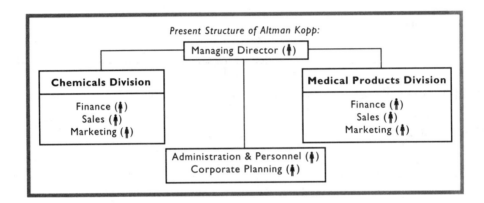

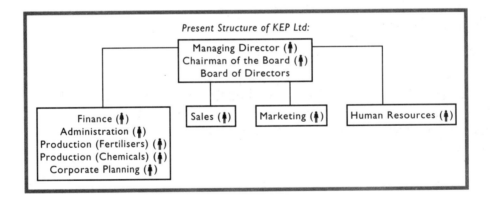

YOU:

- **want to keep the basic structure of your present company, but would like to enlarge it to take in the new product areas that your potential partners specialize in**

- **plan to reduce the number of Altman Kopp directors from the present eight to five or six**

- **want approximately equal representation on the new board but would accept fewer board members if the Chairman of the Board is from your company**

- **want to reduce your present Marketing and Sales Departments to a single department**

- **want to create a new Logistics Department instead of Corporate Planning**

- **know that the Head of Personnel and Administration, who is also on the Board, is retiring.**

YOU START.

© Penguin Books 1996

(Questioning; sequencing)

Trade fairs are opportunities for individuals and companies to make contacts with potential customers and other professionals in the industry. While many companies hope to sign up orders for goods, most are happy to improve consumer awareness of the company and to promote the corporate image.

You are at a trade fair. Introduce your company to someone who visits your stand. Use the following profile as a source of key facts about your company.

Roberto/a Zoff

Deputy Vice-President – Marketing

CONTA (Florida) Limited Roosevelt Building

120–124 24th Street Tampa FL33660–0047

Tel (1) 813 54679900

Name:	CONTA Inc.
Sector:	Property development
Markets:	Japan, South Korea, Singapore, Malaysia, Taiwan, Philippines, USA.
199– Sales:	$93.3m
Hotel/leisure:	$20.25m (21.7%)
Management services:	$7.5m (8.0%)
Engineering:	$15.05m (16.1%)
Property trading:	$1.45m (1.6%)
Property investment:	$49.05m (52.6%)

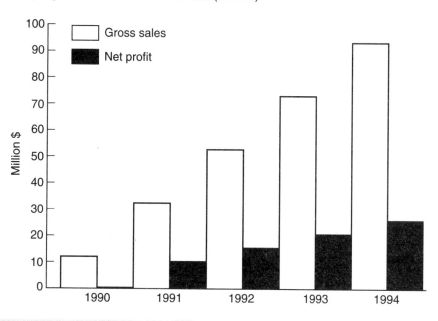

Be prepared to add other information about the location of head office (Osaka), the number of overseas subsidiaries (eight) and the number of direct employees (890). Then ask the other person about his/her company. Ask about:

- **company name, turnover, markets, sales growth**
- **name/location of American subsidiary**
- **number of employees in USA**
- **sales of USA subsidiary**
- **if the company was recently involved in a major takeover.**

Interrupt to ask for clarification or additional information whenever you like.

Note:
As an alternative, present your own company.

YOUR PARTNER WILL START.

    © Penguin Books 1996

15 COMPANY TOUR

(Greetings and farewells; sequencing; questioning, welcoming)

Showing a visitor round your company can be a useful way of winning customers as well as promoting the image of your company.

You work for a manufacturer of sweets and chocolates, a subsidiary of a major US food company. You are going to show an important potential client (your partner) round your company. Before you go round, make a short presentation of the main features of the tour, using the plan below. Your visitor (your partner) has a copy of the same plan.

Start by telling your visitor very briefly about the company's main products, its history and its organization. Then talk through the tour which you are about to make. You want to impress your visitor with the quality of your products, the sophistication of your technology and the good morale of your staff.

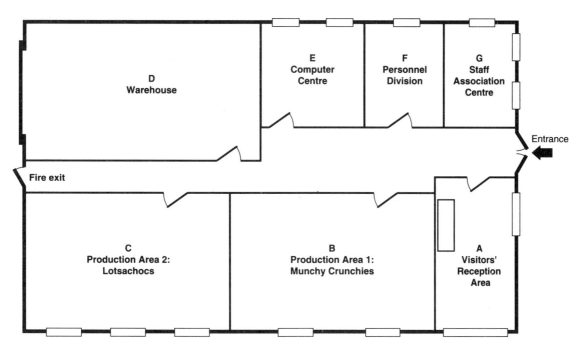

Mention during your initial presentation:

A This is where you are now: the product range.
B A million Munchy Crunchies (chocolate-coated biscuits) per day produced here.
C Your medium-range box of milk chocolates – Lotsachocs – produced and packed here.
D Warehouse: in the process of being fully automated.
E Computer centre: company's local area networks and direct links with the US managed from here.
F Personnel: includes mini-hospital, managed by company doctor, and company health and fitness centre; you are very proud of your policies on health, safety and welfare.
G Very active: numerous sports clubs and leisure time activities for employees, their families and retired members.

Tell your partner that you'll be happy to answer questions during your talk. Remember that this is only an introduction to the tour you are about to make.

YOU START.

16 COMPANY VISIT

(Questioning; regretting)

Before you visit a company, it is useful to check with the person you are visiting about how to get in. Some companies, for example those involved in defence, can have strict security procedures which you need to know about in advance.

You work in a large company which sometimes does top secret research for the government. At the moment there are worries about losing these contracts and about spying, and security is tight. You are looking forward to receiving a visit tomorrow from someone you met recently at a trade fair and have already sent the fax below. You are about to call your contact for the information you need when you receive a call.

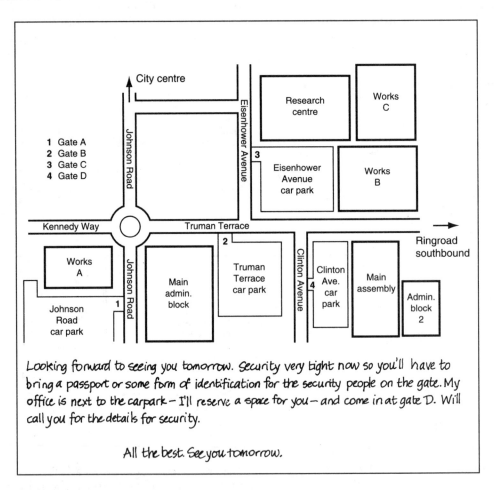

Looking forward to seeing you tomorrow. Security very tight now so you'll have to bring a passport or some form of identification for the security people on the gate. My office is next to the car park – I'll reserve a space for you – and come in at gate D. Will call you for the details for security.

All the best. See you tomorrow.

YOU NEED TO KNOW:

- **your contact's full name and company name**
- **the car registration number and type of car so that you can reserve a space**
- **what kind of identification your contact will bring: passport, identity card . . . (it has to have a photo) and the number.**

You are embarrassed about having to ask for all these details. Say you'll fax the number of the parking space by the end of the day.

YOUR PARTNER WILL START.

© Penguin Books 1996

(Agreeing/disagreeing; forecasting; hesitating)

The culture of a company is the set of beliefs, values, attitudes and organizational characteristics which make it unique. Some managers and business observers believe that changing the culture of an organization is the best way to significantly improve its business performance.

You and your partner woke up this morning to find yourselves joint heads of a large international company. Unfortunately, it is losing a lot of money. You both feel that a major transformation of the culture of the company is needed and you have brainstormed ten possible policies below. Now go through the list and decide together which ones you will implement.

1   You – the joint managing directors – should give up your big offices on the top floor and establish your base by the main photocopier on the ground floor.

2   Abolish individual pay, introduce pay based on team performance.

3   Aim for 50% of managers to be women within the next two years. (At the moment 60% of your employees and 5% of your senior managers are women.)

4   Abolish 'senior' management. Reduce the number of layers in the organization as far as possible.

5   Abolish the Personnel Department.

6   Make all managers fly economy class.

7   Abolish company cars. Pay people an allowance when they have to drive on company business.

8   Make all employees – yourselves included – wear a company uniform.

9   Make meetings shorter, have everyone stand up.

10 Instead of managers appraising subordinates, get subordinates to appraise managers.

You may come up with your own ideas as well.

YOU START.

© Penguin Books 1996

(Forecasting; judging; urging; negotiating)

Corporate sponsorship is big business. Companies give money to sporting, cultural and charitable organizations as a way of bringing the company's name and products to the attention of a wider public.

Your company has decided to spend a large sum of money on some kind of sponsorship. You and your partner have been made responsible for recommending the best option to the Board. You have shortlisted three possible organizations you could sponsor. The cost of each option is approximately the same. You are now in a meeting with your partner to decide on the best option.

FILE 1

The football club in the city where your company is based has just lost its sponsor after going down from the national first to the second division at the end of the last season. Now the club is desperately looking for a replacement. The manager has been sacked and replaced by a well-known ex-international player with no previous managerial experience. There are no new players in the team. The club has large debts. Advanced sales of season tickets are poor and some people are saying that the number of spectators next season could be 20% down on last year. However, sponsorship would give your company excellent opportunities for advertising the company logo on the team shirt, in the weekly match programme and around the ground. You can expect two or three home matches to be televised live during the season. There are also good opportunities for corporate hospitality at home matches.

FILE 2

The government has reduced the grant it normally gives to your local city orchestra which as a result will have to disband if it is unable to find money from another source. In fact, you have already been approached by a committee of local art lovers, including some representatives from the city council, seeking your help. The orchestra currently does not have a permanent conductor. The average age of the players (who are employed on a part-time basis) is 49. The orchestra normally gives six to eight concerts per year, almost always in the Town Hall and another two or three during the city's annual cultural festival. One or two of these concerts might be broadcast on national radio each year. The orchestra has a regional rather than a national reputation but has traditionally been central to local cultural life. Some people say its programmes are too conservative: it rarely plays twentieth century music. Sponsorship would put your company name on concert programmes and on all promotional literature. You would have free tickets for all concerts to offer to clients and prospective customers.

   © Penguin Books 1996

FILE 3

Your city is the base for a young troupe of dancers who, in a short period of time, have gained a reputation for exciting choreography and innovative technique. One national newspaper critic hailed them as 'the most exciting development in modern ballet in the last twenty years.' The troupe is especially popular with young people: some of their most enthusiastic fans had never previously been to a performance of ballet. So far they have managed on a shoestring budget but are now receiving invitations to perform elsewhere in the country and even abroad, and they need money to invest in rehearsal rooms, to pay an administration manager, and so on. At the moment they have no permanent headquarters. The troupe are now actively looking for a sponsor and would be willing to incorporate the sponsor's name into their own name. Their activities are not, however, without controversy: there have been complaints about political bias in the themes presented in the dancing and some people have been shocked at what they see on the stage. You know that one of the Board members is unhappy about his teenage children attending their performances. On the other hand, you have been advised privately that the troupe could have an international reputation within the next ten years.

YOUR PARTNER WILL START.

19 COSTS AND REDUCING OVERHEADS

(Judging; emphasizing; forecasting)

Costs include production costs and the costs of selling. All aspects of a company's expenditure should be recorded as costs and good management aims to keep costs to a minimum within an agreed budget.

You work for a subsidiary of an international company. Your head office has sent instructions that costs should be reduced by 10% next year.

Discuss the following options with a colleague and decide which options you would introduce to meet the required savings.

- lay off 100 workers out of a total of 1,000 (5% saving)
- lay off 50 workers (2.5% saving)
- import more raw materials instead of buying from domestic suppliers (2% saving)
- use low energy lighting in non-essential areas of the plant (1% saving)
- reduce heating from 25°C to 22°C (2% saving)
- abandon plans to upgrade existing successful product range (3.5% saving)
- cut dividend to shareholders by 1% (2% saving)
- employ contractors to maintain equipment (2% saving).

YOU:

- **are very keen to develop the company in the medium and long term**

- **know that the market is very competitive and customers are easily attracted to competitors' products**

- **are sensitive to employees' opinions and wishes**

- **think that the company should not reduce its workforce**

- **think the company should not change to using contractors for routine work, especially where maintenance is concerned and safety could be affected**

- **realize you will have to compromise on some of these ideas.**

YOUR PARTNER WILL START.

© Penguin Books 1996

(Questioning; judging)

Customer care is knowing your customers, knowing what they want, reacting to their changing needs, and keeping close to them. It is important for all members of business organizations to think about who their customers are and how they can improve their service to them.

Your partner is a work colleague who is part of a special task force set up by top management to improve customer care throughout the company. The first job of the task force is to find out how customer-conscious staff members think the company is at the moment. (Later on, employee perceptions of customer attitudes will be compared with customer attitudes themselves.)

Your partner is going to ask you questions from a customer attitude survey to find out how you think customers rate your organization's current performance.

YOU:

• **answer the questions with reference to your own organization.**

YOUR PARTNER WILL START.

© Penguin Books 1996

(Blaming; judging; negotiating; declining/rejecting)

When a customer complains, it is important to resolve the problem as quickly and courteously as possible.

You are the customer relations manager for a British company offering package skiing holidays. You have received a letter of complaint from a dissatisfied customer.

```
                                            23 Pennylong Avenue
                                            London NW2 5PG


27 February 199-

Customer Relations Manager
Super Skibreak Holidays
27 Porthill Road
Oxford OX4 2AR

Holiday receipt number FSB/403994/02/18

Dear Sir/Madam,

I have just returned from one of your so-called "February
skiing breaks" extremely disappointed with your company's
service for the following reasons.
1 The two-star hotel described in your brochure as a
  "comfortable family-run hotel" in fact offered only
  basic facilities and was dirty. The food was poor.
2 Your brochure also says that "if insufficient snow in
  your resort causes lifts and/or ski school to close,
  we'll do our best to arrange free coach transport to
  another resort where skiing is possible." Although
  skiing conditions were so poor on three days out of
  six that the skiing was unsafe, as your own local
  representative himself admitted, we were not provided
  with the transportation promised.
The quality of this holiday was so bad that I feel that
you should refund me the whole cost of the holiday. I
should therefore be grateful if you would arrange for me
to receive the sum of £691.40 as soon as possible. If I
do not receive a satisfactory reply within seven days, I
shall take legal advice.

Yours faithfully

J. Cameron

J. Cameron
```

© Penguin Books 1996

You have talked to the local representative who says:

1 that the hotel is indeed family-run and is usually appreciated for its friendliness. This usually compensates for its fairly basic facilities. Unfortunately there was a serious flu epidemic in February which led to staff shortages – hence the problems with the food. The customer did not mention hotel problems to the rep.

2 although the snow was not good, there was no question of the lifts or ski school closing. Most of the other holiday makers would have missed half or one day's skiing at most because of the conditions. Your rep. denies admitting that the conditions were very poor on three days out of six.

Call the customer (your partner) to resolve the problem.

YOU:

- **feel that the claim for a total refund of £691.40 is unjustified although you are prepared to pay some compensation**

- **want to satisfy your customer's demands and convince him/her of your commitment to good customer relations – at minimum cost to your company.**

YOU START.

22 CUSTOMS HOLDUP

(Questioning; urging; expressing amazement; regretting)

Frontier delays are usually caused by errors in the documentation accompanying goods. Occasionally other problems arise where the goods in a particular consignment do not match the description given to customs authorities.

You are a director of a manufacturing company, Allen Deal Inc. One of your drivers has been arrested at an international frontier with a consignment of printed circuit boards and other components that he was bringing to your factory. The delivery is vital for a major contract that is already behind schedule. Contact the customs authority at the frontier and find out:

- the reason for the delay
- what is happening to the driver
- when the lorry can continue its journey.

YOU:

- **desperately need the components to be allowed to continue the journey at once – a massive $1.5m contract is dependent on work being completed within a few days. A holdup will make this impossible**

- **cannot leave your office today – you are due to meet an important customer this afternoon**

- **know that the managing director went into hospital last week, suffering from stress**

- **know that if the company does not complete the order on time, the contract will be lost and the company will have to sack 100 workers**

- **have heard that this country frequently stops lorries at its frontier and there is a rumour that the customs officials are corrupt. You don't know if this is true . . .**

YOU START.

 © Penguin Books 1996

23 EMPLOYEE MORALE

Student A

(Urging; sequencing; agreeing/disagreeing)

Many companies are reducing the size of the workforce, while at the same time expecting their employees to provide a high level of customer care. Maintaining the morale of the staff is both difficult and necessary, and is becoming more and more a central management challenge.

You and your partner, in the Human Resources department of a company which is in the process of reducing its workforce by 20%, meet to devise a strategy to ensure that employee morale remains as high as possible during the period of downsizing.

Tell your partner about the following list of five strategic actions which you have drawn up. Your partner will also tell you about the points which he or she has noted. Then, together, choose the five key actions for your strategy in order of priority.

YOU want to:

1. **introduce an annual employee opinion survey with responsibility for analysis of results and implementation of actions held by the Director of Human Resources**

2. **introduce weekly team briefing systems for all employees**

3. **create a suggestions scheme with attractive financial rewards for prize-winning suggestions**

4. **have all staff attend a series of seminars led by senior management explaining the business objectives of the company**

5. **provide an in-house counselling service to deal with problems of employee stress.**

YOUR PARTNER WILL START.

(Greetings and farewells; introducing self and others; questioning; welcoming; sequencing)

Corporate entertainment is often an important part of building good relations with business partners. Entertainment may be formal and highly planned, involving prominent people from the company or the region; in other cases, entertainment may be more personal and informal.

You are about to receive a visitor from another city or country who has come to your home town for the first time. You telephone him/her to plan a fairly detailed entertainment package, lasting three days. After this time, you plan to begin some informal business discussions.

YOU:

- **should outline some ideas on how your visitor could spend the three days**
- **find out what would interest your visitor**
- **learn what he/she likes to do to relax**
- **try to work out a fairly detailed itinerary with your visitor.**

Remember – after three days you have to start informal discussions about business.

YOU START.

When you have finished, your partner invites you to visit his/her home town in return. You accept!

YOUR PARTNER WILL START.

© Penguin Books 1996

(Sequencing; urging; agreeing/disagreeing)

More and more companies are becoming concerned about the effect their activities have on the natural environment. Some companies are carrying out environmental audits, others are publishing environmental accounts which try to measure this impact. There is no doubt that this will become a major activity of companies in the future.

As part of a campaign to make your company more environmentally friendly, you and your colleague have been made responsible for improving the environmental balance in the office block where you both work.

Look together at the following suggestions and prioritize them.

---

1 Separate waste bins for paper and plastics.

2 Separate waste bins for batteries (before recycling).

3 Separate waste bins for newspapers and magazines (before recycling).

4 Separate waste bins for glass (before recycling).

5 Use of recycled paper for the photocopier.

6 An indoor plant on every desk.

7 A daily record sheet for all photocopies made.

8 A daily photocopying quota per department to reduce by 25% the number of photocopies made.

9 A policy of turning off all electric lights in unoccupied rooms.

10 Punishment of employees who leave lights on in unoccupied rooms.

11 Use of low energy light bulbs throughout the building.

12 Reduction of the temperature by 5°C throughout the building.

13 Installation of double glazing throughout.

14 Incentives to encourage employees to travel to work by public transport rather than by car.

15 Any other suggestions which you and your partner can offer to make your offices more environmentally friendly places.

YOU START.

© Penguin Books 1996

(Agreeing/disagreeing; correcting; liking and preferring)

Equal opportunities is an area where many companies and many states have rules or legislation designed to protect specific groups from discrimination or unfair treatment. Such areas as terms of contract, wages and salaries, career prospects, job security and working conditions are affected by equal opportunities policies.

You are part of a discussion group which must produce recommendations to the Board on ways to improve the position of women in the company.

Note that:

- **58% of the 400 company employees are women**
- **only 5% of management positions are held by women**
- **the company has no policy on encouraging women to return to work after maternity leave, consequently only a very small number do return**
- **the Chairman has said he wants to improve the position of women in the company.**

In discussion with a colleague, prioritize the following suggestions (from the most important to the least important) to create an enlightened and progressive policy for employment.

- Actively encourage women to return to work after taking maternity leave. ☐
- Improve internal training opportunities, encouraging women to apply for internal promotions. ☐
- Encourage more part-time work, job-sharing, etc. with full employee rights. ☐
- Introduce flexible time-tabling (flexitime). ☐
- Provide crêche facilities. ☐
- Improve maternity leave with full job security. ☐
- Set a quota for female representation in management positions. ☐
- Corporate statement on sexual harassment to be included in employment conditions. ☐
- A promise from management to investigate reports of sexual harassment immediately. ☐
- More liberal attitude towards women's choice of clothing. ☐

YOUR PARTNER WILL START.

© Penguin Books 1996

(Judging; knowing; hesitating; correcting; declining/rejecting)

Franchising is running a business which appears to be part of a chain of similar businesses, each with the same name, image and ethos, similar products and a similar marketing strategy. A franchisee pays a franchisor a fee and in return gets advice and support on how to run the business.

You are the manager of a franchised fast food outlet in a medium-sized town. Your relationship with the franchisor, Eet Up, is not very good. You have scheduled a meeting with an Eet Up representative to try to sort out some problems.

In preparation for the meeting you have written the following letter, which lists key points in order of importance to you. You should aim to achieve some, but not all, of the improvements listed. Your hand-written notes to yourself are added, showing your thoughts.

```
A. Cook
Area Manager (Franchise Agreements)
Eet Up
Park Grove
London SW15 2RT                          22 November 19—

Dear Mr Cook,
Following our recent conversation, I write to confirm the
points for discussion at our meeting next month. I would like
to talk about the following changes to our present agreement
which is due for renewal in the Spring of next year:
  - a reduction in the franchise fee from the present $50,000
    per year  $40-45,000 — key point!!!
  - a 50% grant towards the costs of developing the site.
    Increasing seating from 120 to 200.
  - freedom to buy ingredients locally. Save 10%
  - Eet Up to run more on-site staff training.  It's been bad
  - preparation of a quarterly business report to Eet Up,
    not monthly.
  - Eet Up to sponsor special promotions, such as
    combinations with theatres, cinemas, clubs, etc.
  - Eet Up to send more information on market trends.

Looking forward to a successful meeting,

Best regards,

Steve Bailey
Steve Bailey
```

YOU:

- **want to remain with Eet Up**
- **think the expansion of your business should bring more benefits to you, rather than to the franchisor.**

YOU START.

28 HEALTH AND SAFETY

(Obliging; permitting; emphasizing; urging)

Companies are controlled by legislation affecting health and safety. In addition, many have their own policies to ensure that health and safety issues are constantly monitored and improved where necessary.

Your company has a very bad record on health and safety. Employee representatives and government officials have demanded immediate improvements; otherwise the company may be forced to close.

You have a meeting with a colleague to discuss ways to improve the situation.

The following is an extract from a report on incidents concerning health and safety in recent months.

January 12:	Casual worker electrocuted by faulty wiring.
February 15:	Fork lift accident – worker hospitalized. The operator was not qualified to use a fork lift.
February 17:	Worker falls off a roof while carrying out a repair.
April 4:	Chemical leak from a faulty waste pipe.
May 19:	Chemical leak: undiluted chlorine agents polluted nearby river.
July 2:	Roof blown off storage depot in a storm. Two workers injured.
August 23:	Fire on a rubbish tip.
September 2:	Night security man attacked by intruder. Not discovered for two hours. Received hospital treatment.
October 16:	Lorry crashes in despatch area. Witnesses say driver was going too fast. A lot of damage caused to vehicle: driver unhurt.

YOU:

- **want immediate decisions on what must be done and a firm date for implementing any changes**
- **think that cost is not the issue as failure to improve matters will result in the closure of the factory**
- **know that the government is planning much stricter rules on health and safety, including powers to fine companies which allow accidents to happen**
- **want an end to using untrained, casual labour**
- **want a detailed training programme established to improve workers' awareness of safety issues**
- **think that a better trained, full-time workforce would improve both safety and productivity**
- **think that maintenance and house-keeping on site could be improved without incurring major costs, e.g. by improving disposal of waste products.**

YOUR PARTNER WILL START.

 © Penguin Books 1996

29 IN-HOUSE MAGAZINE
(Agreeing/disagreeing; liking and preferring; measuring and calculating)

An in-house magazine can be an important tool for internal communication. It can serve to inform staff members of important company developments and encourage them to identify with corporate objectives.

You and your partner are members of a small task force formed to upgrade your company's in-house journal. You have been given a free hand to draw up a set of recommendations to submit to senior management.

You must:

- **identify the objectives of the magazine**
- **decide on how often the magazine should appear**
- **decide on the page size, number of pages and general look**
- **think of a name**
- **draw up a budget for a magazine with a circulation of 5,000 (editorial, design and production costs).**

For the content, decide which of the following you think should or should not appear in each issue:

- **a message from the Chairman of the company**
- **recent sales figures**
- **other financial information relating to the company's performance**
- **news and photographs of new recruits**
- **news and photographs of recent retirements**
- **features presenting individual employees**
- **features presenting the work of individual departments**
- **company sports news, social club news, news from the company's various clubs and associations**
- **interviews with senior executives**
- **trade union news**
- **a summary of coverage of the company and its products in the national and specialized press**
- **future plans for expanding or contracting the workforce**
- **recent acquisitions, joint venture agreements**
- **recent product launches, news of future product plans.**

Can you think of anything else which should be included?

YOU START.

(Judging; agreeing/disagreeing)

Interviewing technique affects both the style of an interview and the type of questions asked. Many interviews use a combination of approaches to discover as much as possible about the applicant.

Look at the following job advertisement:

MARKETING MANAGER

An expanding young software development company with 950 employees, with its head office in London and with production sites in London, Rotterdam and Paris, is looking for a dynamic, ambitious graduate with experience in direct selling and strategic planning, preferably in a relevant sector.

Telephone 0800 5656 and ask for Freephone Professional for further details and an application form.

With your partner, classify the following interview questions into three groups: Personal/Psychological (PP), Academic and Professional Background (AP), Hypothetical (H). Then assess them on a scale of 1 to 5: where 1 = most useful in a job interview, and 5 = not useful at all. Give reasons for your assessments.

1 Can you give an example of a situation where you have been in conflict with colleagues in your present job or in a previous job?
2 Do you enjoy working alone or do you prefer teamwork?
3 How does your experience until now prepare you for the work in this company?
4 How does your family feel about your relocation to London?
5 Given your lack of experience in software development – your background is in the food sector – is this likely to be a problem?
6 What do you do when you need to relax?
7 If a product you were responsible for was obviously failing in a particular market, what would you do to resolve the situation?
8 How do you see the future of the computing industry in ten years' time?
9 Can you describe a particular project that you have been closely involved with in your present job?

YOU START.

      © Penguin Books 1996

A job application is a formal request for a job. You usually make an application by replying to an advertisement. People who apply for a job are job applicants.

You are the personal assistant to a well-known film director, planning to leave for a well-earned rest after five years in the post. You placed the job advertisement below in the national press and received several good applications, including a very interesting one from your partner. Although you acknowledged this some weeks ago, you have been too busy to invite him/her to interview. You now receive a call from him/her to find out what is happening and to get more information about the job. You can tell the applicant (your partner) about:

- **travel: you travel constantly, to all parts of the world, and are away on location sometimes for months at a time**

- **hours: from 0 to 24 hours per day – there are no typical working hours**

- **pay: the base salary is nothing special, the performance-related element is related to the success of the latest film**

- **problems: living out of suitcases, the director's terrible temper, actors and actresses who fall ill, etc. . . .**

You can invent other details about the job but you are not at liberty to reveal the director's name.

In turn, you would like some more information about this applicant:

- **languages spoken?**
- **typing?**
- **driving licence?**
- **tough?**
- **adaptable?**
- **can get on well with all sorts of people?**
- **experience?**
- **available as from when?**
- **plus other questions of your own.**

HELP! MY PA IS LEAVING ME!

In fact, we're parting on good terms after five years but I need a replacement FAST. If you've got what it takes to be PA to a well-known film director, write to Box XPA/475 at this newspaper now. Good salary (performance-related).

No previous film industry experience required.

> ### MEGA MEDIA ENTERTAINMENT
>
> ....
>
> 71 Gracechurch Street
> London N1 1QA
> Tel: 0171 222 7548 Fax: 0171 358 6037
>
> **Berlin – London – Paris – New York – Rome – San Francisco**
>
> Thank you for your recent application for the
> advertised post. You will hear from us very
> shortly.
>
> Yours sincerely,
>
> *Linda Devito*
> Linda Devito

YOUR PARTNER WILL START.

32 LARGE VERSUS SMALL COMPANIES

Student A

(Liking and preferring; judging; correcting)

A company's workforce may range in size from one employee to tens of thousands of people. Some people prefer to work in small companies, others prefer to be part of a large organization.

In this activity, you are going to debate with your partner the advantages of working for large and small companies. You prefer small companies, your partner prefers large. Use the arguments below to help you win the argument. Add your own arguments to the discussion.

YOU believe the following arguments:

1 In a small company, you know everyone. Small companies are friendlier. It's good to be able to get to know the people you work with really well.

2 In small companies, you can sort out problems face-to-face.

3 There's more variety to your work in a small company. You have to be ready to turn your hand to more or less anything.

4 You are more independent in a small company. When you want to do something, you don't have to wait for permission from all kinds of people above you.

5 When you work for a small company, you feel proud of making a direct contribution to the success of the organization.

6 People who work in big companies are too ready to conform.

7 You know where you are in a small company: you're not afraid that you'll suddenly lose your job without warning.

8 The advantages of working in a small company are freedom, flexibility and openness.

9 You've got more chance of realizing your full potential in a small company.

You also think that . . .

YOUR PARTNER WILL START.

(Urging; emphasizing; negotiating)

Cashflow considerations may sometimes create difficulties where naturally one company wants immediate payment but the other prefers to delay as long as possible.

It is now January 7th. Your company sent the following invoice five weeks ago, plus a reminder a week ago. You have still not received payment.

KWAN SERVICES

450–58 Jalan Bukit Bintang
55100 Kuala Lumpur, Malaysia
Telephone (03) 77878779   Fax (03) 77878562

INVOICE

Arndale Promotions
112 Depot Row
PO Box 4567
Auckland, New Zealand

2 December 199–

Ref. Your order dated 24 September
Singapore Market Analysis Consultancy Report

Fee:	$US4,000
Expenses:	$US 567

TOTAL NOW DUE	$US4,567

Bank details:
KWAN Services Current account No. 70852406
Branch Sorting Code: 20-99-56
Credit Bank International,
Jelan Melaka 200, Kuala Lumpur, Malaysia.
Terms:
30 days from date of invoice.

Telephone Arndale Promotions.

YOU:

- **have a serious cashflow problem**
- **urgently need payment**
- **remind your partner of the terms stated on your invoice.**

YOU START.

34 MANAGEMENT AND LEADERSHIP SKILLS FOR WOMEN

Student A

(Urging; negotiating; agreeing/disagreeing)

Companies and training organizations are increasingly offering courses especially for women, for example in leadership skills and assertiveness, in order to help women increase their self-confidence and their belief in their own ideas and actions in professional and personal situations.

You and your partner are helping with the design of a new training programme which will eventually be followed by all female employees who are managers or who have management potential, as part of the company's overall employee development programme.

You have identified five problem areas to look at during the course.

1 Dealing with a team member who is not pulling his or her weight.

2 Handling former colleagues who are jealous of your success.

3 Managing employees who are older than you.

4 Managing men.

5 Supervising a close friend.

Decide with your partner:

- **the best way to handle these problems**

- **a training idea (role play, simulation, game, discussion, case study . . .) to help the course participants to learn how to handle each situation better.**

YOUR PARTNER WILL START.

© Penguin Books 1996

(Sequencing; judging; agreeing/disagreeing)

It is difficult to find universal agreement on the specific personality and professional characteristics which make a good manager. Team building usually aims to cover a range of qualities as one individual cannot have all the positive management attributes.

Discuss the following characteristics of what makes a good manager and, with your partner, rank them in order of importance:

- ability to get on well with colleagues ☐
- technical knowledge ☐
- experience of management in different industrial sectors ☐
- ability to make people laugh ☐
- willingness to work up to 60 hours a week ☐
- confidence in making decisions ☐
- concern for well-being of every employee from the top to the bottom of an organization ☐
- ability to understand details of company activity ☐
- ability to plan and understand corporate objectives ☐
- knowledge of the world ☐
- highly educated and cultured individual with wide range of personal interests ☐
- commitment to making money ☐
- stable health and psychological make-up ☐
- supportive family ☐
- ability to motivate ☐
- ability to delegate ☐

YOUR PARTNER WILL START.

© Penguin Books 1996

(Questioning; liking and preferring)

Companies sometimes employ external consultants to carry out market research to help them target products and services better. Some market research is very useful, but the techniques used to gather information have to be carefully designed.

Your company owns a chain of hotels and restaurants. You receive a market research report from an agency which has investigated guests' opinions in some of your hotels.

PRELIMINARY REPORT

Number of respondents: 1,147

Survey technique: Customers staying in your hotels were asked to complete a form which was left in hotel rooms.

Analysis by purpose of visit:
Business: 78%   Private/tourism: 22%

Analysis by duration of visit:
One night: 48%   2 nights: 33%   3 nights: 10%   More than 3 nights: 9%

Analysis by services used:
Bed & Breakfast only: 65%   Evening meal: 35%

Quality Assessment:
1 = outstanding   2 = very good   3 = average   4 = poor   5 = very bad

Welcome on arrival:	2.5
Quality of service at reception:	2.1
Facilities available from reception:	3.0
Rooms, comfort, decor, etc.:	2.4
Beds:	3.0
Room service:	2.6
Value for money:	3.4
Breakfast:	2.8
Dinner/restaurant:	2.9

YOU:

- **are not happy with the survey**
- **think it needs much more detailed information to be useful, for example: what does it mean to say the welcome on arrival was rated 2.5? How could it be improved? What do customers expect?**
- **also want to know what needs to be done to improve the beds, if they are rated only as average?**
- **want to know how relevant it is that the survey respondents were self-selected, i.e. they chose to fill in the forms. What percentage of guests actually completed the forms?**
- **want to know what variation there was between different hotels in the group.**

YOU START.

(Questioning; liking and preferring)

Market research is the activity of collecting information about consumers and what consumers want and need. This information is used to help produce the goods and services which will ensure success for the company.

You work for a market research organization. You want to find out more information about consumer needs in the camera market. You are out on the street conducting interviews using the following questionnaire.

Introduce yourself and explain what you are doing. Then, if your partner agrees to help, ask the questions. Fill in his/her answers on the form.

AUDIO VISUAL EQUIPMENT
MARKET SURVEY – SECTOR: CAMERAS

1 Do you own a camera?   YES/NO

2 If YES, how old is it?
   a) less than 1 yr   b) 1–2 yrs   c) 2–3 yrs   d) more than 3 yrs
   If NO go on to question 5.

3 What make is it?
   CANON/KODAK/MINOLTA/NIKON/OLYMPUS/PANASONIC/PRAKTIKA/SONY/ZENITH/other (please state).

4 How much did it cost?
   a) less than $150   b) $151–250   c) $251–350   d) more than $350

5 Do you plan to buy a camera in the next year?   YES/NO

6 How much do you plan to spend?
   a) less than $150   b) $151–250   c) $251–350   d) more than $350

7 Which make(s) of camera do you think are the best value for money?
   CANON/KODAK/MINOLTA/NIKON/OLYMPUS/PANASONIC/PRAKTIKA/SONY/ZENITH/don't know/other (please state)

8 How many rolls of film do you normally use in a year?
   a) fewer than 5   b) 6–10   c) 11–20   d) more than 20

Name of respondent: _____

Age: Under 16   16–18   19–24   25–30   31–45   46–60   Over 60

Marital status: single   married   divorced   separated

Address: _____

_____

Date: _____   Time: _____

Finally, ask for the respondent's name and address. If he/she gives you this information, his/her name will automatically be placed in a prize draw. The first prize is a two-week holiday in the Seychelles.

YOU START.

     © Penguin Books 1996

38 MEETING ARRANGEMENTS

(Obliging; declining/rejecting; urging; judging)

One definition of a meeting is: the gathering together of a group of people for a controlled discussion with a specific purpose. The essential elements of a meeting are:

- *a purpose: problem-solving, idea-gathering or training*
- *an agenda: the list of points to be discussed*
- *the members: the chairperson, the secretary and the other members*
- *a result: the outcome of the process*
- *a report: usually the minutes (written by the secretary).*

Your company exports its electrical goods around the world. Unfortunately one of your overseas agents is not selling many of your products. You want a meeting next week to discuss ways to improve sales. Telephone your agent to ask for a meeting.

YOU:

- **think a meeting is absolutely necessary to relaunch the partnership**
- **want to show a video about new selling methods used by your company**
- **want to discuss sales performance, looking at graphs and other illustrations**
- **want the meeting next week!**
- **have heard that your partner is doing very well selling other products.**

Here are your appointments for next week:

13 Monday Department Meeting 10 a.m.	**16 Thursday**
14 Tuesday	**17 Friday**
15 Wednesday Show training video to regional sales team	**18 Saturday**
	19 Sunday

YOU START.

(Knowing; judging; urging; sequencing; permitting)

A mission statement is a statement of the aims, purpose and future activities of an organization. The objective of the mission statement is to define – for the company's employees, its customers and its shareholders – what kind of organization it is, what it believes in, and in which direction it wants to go.

You and your partner both work for the same international company. You have been given the job of producing an effective mission statement for your company. Your task is to draft a first version of the statement for circulation, about a dozen sentences long.

Your draft could include statements about:

- **the usefulness of the company's products and services in the community**
- **the company's objectives**
- **the company's values**
- **the company's policies on quality and on customer care**
- **the company's principles on personnel**
- **the company's policy on the environment and towards the countries of the developing world**
- **anything else you think is important.**

YOU START.

© Penguin Books 1996

(Negotiating; declining/rejecting; urging)

Most employees get some benefits from their employer in addition to their basic pay. Some senior managers receive very generous fringe benefits from their companies, which together are worth much more than the salary alone. Some people prefer to receive just money for the work they do; others prefer to receive pay plus other kinds of benefit. The total of what you receive is called your remuneration package.

In this exercise, you play the role of a personnel manager talking to your partner who is an executive in the company where you both work. Until now, the company has offered its more senior managers a wide range of benefits in addition to basic salary. Now, however, the company wants to cut the range of benefits being offered and wants to bring earnings under tighter control. Look at the information below and discuss with your partner how his or her remuneration package can be altered.

Current package per annum

Base salary	£20,000
Performance-related bonus last year	£10,650
(Note: maximum possible PRB was	£20,000)
Company car and private use of petrol	£3,600
Long-term disability cover	£1,500
Subsidized lunches	£1,250
Employer contributions to company pension fund	£1,200
Private medical insurance	£1,200
Parking	£950
Life assurance	£300
Annual health screening	£200
Financial planning	£200
Health club membership	£150
Total	**£41,200**

YOU:

- **want to keep the new package as close to £40,000 as possible, and preferably below it, unless justified by performance**

- **are empowered to increase the performance-related element of the package according to your judgement, but you cannot increase basic salary by more than 25%**

- **want to reduce your administration costs and therefore want to minimize the number of fringe benefits you offer**

- **want to keep your managers happy.**

YOU START.

(Emphasizing; blaming; telling; expressing your fear/worry; vetoing)

Evaluation and appraisal are used to ensure that employees develop their full potential within the company. Accurate assessment is vital in determining pay, career development and the company's commitment to individuals.

You are a manager in a production company. You have a meeting with a colleague to discuss an employee who is doing badly at work. Last week he failed to arrive on Monday and Tuesday, he was late on Thursday and on Friday he incorrectly completed work record forms.

Here is an internal report on the employee involved:

EMPLOYEE PERFORMANCE EVALUATION & HEALTH REPORT
STRICTLY CONFIDENTIAL

Name: John Casenove
Sex: M
Position: Line operator/Chargehand

History
John Casenove joined the company three years ago. For eighteen months his record was above average, with a good level of performance, low absenteeism and excellent inter-personal relations. He was promoted to chargehand 18 months ago.

   For six months he responded well to the promotion and continued to be a valued employee.

Recent problems
Casenove began to arrive late for work and was frequently absent. A supervisor's report said he appeared depressed and uninterested. He was offered counselling by the company counselling service. The offer was refused.

   Three months ago he was disciplined for assaulting a colleague. He was fined one week's wages. He was warned as to his future conduct.

YOU:

- **are tired of the problems surrounding Mr Casenove**
- **think the company has every justification for giving him the sack**
- **think the minimum action should be to replace him as chargehand, putting him at a lower level of responsibility.**

YOUR PARTNER WILL START.

 © Penguin Books 1996

42 PRESENTING INFORMATION

Student A

(Sequencing; questioning)

Presenting information is a skill requiring clear organization and concise description. Keep your presentations simple, use short sentences and a clear structure.

Give a three-minute presentation on one of the topics below. You have two minutes to prepare your presentation. At the end your partner will ask you one or two questions.

Then ask your partner to present some information to you. Afterwards, you must ask one or two questions.

Repeat the task with another topic if you like.

Topics:

- **a product you know well**
- **exports from your country**
- **local and national transport**
- **a company you know well**
- **entertainment**

YOUR PARTNER WILL START.

© Penguin Books 1996

(Judging; knowing; agreeing/disagreeing; vetoing)

Public relations is concerned with the image that society in general and customers in particular have of a company. All companies, especially larger ones, are very concerned to develop a good corporate image through their products, services, personnel, brand names and logos. The reputation of a company is formed through attention to all aspects of public relations. Bad publicity of any kind can have serious commercial consequences.

You are a spokesman for a chemicals company, KAD Limited, which is at the centre of a river contamination scandal. You are interviewed by a journalist. Defend your company. Here is an internal report on the incident.

KAD LIMITED
Incident Report

Date of incident: 20/10/19—   **Location: Waste Liquids**

Chlorine, used in the bleaching process, is normally stored in tanks. Later it is removed by a waste disposal company. The chlorine passes from the factory to the tanks through two pipes.

DEFECTIVE JOINT — SOURCE OF LEAK

WASTE LIQUIDS   WASTE LIQUIDS

A defective joint, corroded by rust, caused the above incident. Bleaching agents escaped and were washed away by heavy rain over a weekend. Only security guards were on site. The incident was discovered on Monday when a worker saw the level in the drums was unusually low. The next day local people saw dead fish in the river.

© Penguin Books 1996

YOU:

- think KAD has a good record on health, safety and pollution control
- know that £45,000 was spent on the plant last year – all directly linked to safety and the environment
- say this is the first major incident for fifteen years
- believe KAD is always looking for new ways to protect the environment – within (confidential) cost limits
- are investigating ways to ensure no repetition
- know KAD will pay £5,000 for the clean-up operation
- think many other local companies pollute the river
- know that KAD employs 600 people
- know (confidentially) that KAD is under-insured for industrial pollution accidents.

YOUR PARTNER WILL START.

44 PRODUCT ENDORSEMENT

(Negotiating; forecasting; urging)

When famous people endorse products, they say in advertisements that they approve of them and encourage people to buy them.

You work for an international agency representing leading sports personalities. On your list you have a rising young Swedish tennis star. You are now going to have a meeting with the representative of a sports footwear company (your partner) to discuss the possibility of your tennis player endorsing their goods.

CLIENT FILE

International Sporting Promotions

Name:	Christina Wahlström
Age:	17
Nationality:	Swedish
Profession:	Tennis player
Coach:	Bo Wahlström (father)
Professional:	Swedish Junior Open Champion at 14, Swedish Women's Champion at 16, Wimbledon Quarter Finalist and Australian Semi-Finalist at 17.
Personal:	'The John McEnroe of women's tennis.' Stormy relationships with (i) her father; (ii) numerous boyfriends (iii) tennis umpires.
Potential:	Still developing as a player. Could dominate international women's tennis within three years.

YOU:

- **want a deal worth $1m for your client**
- **are convinced of her tennis potential**
- **think she has great marketing potential: the first Swedish female tennis star**
- **want more information about the product which the footwear company wants her to endorse: it has to have the right image for her and it has to be reliable.**

Persuade your partner of your views.

YOU START.

 © Penguin Books 1996

45 PRODUCTION DELAYS

(Obliging; expressing fear/worry; urging)

Production delays can be caused by many factors from the non-delivery of parts to planning mistakes. The consequences can be small, such as a little internal disruption, or considerable, such as loss of important business.

Your company, DGS Holdings, has a subsidiary in Portugal which produces electronic components for your main production sites in Taiwan and Korea. Unfortunately the Portuguese subsidiary has been having some problems, as shown by the fax below.

> **EUSEBIO TORRES S.A.**
> **PASO DO TOQUINHO 200**
> **TORRES VEDRAS**
> **007893 PORTUGAL**
>
> **FAX: 351 61 324288**
> **TEL: 351 61 567344**
>
> FOR THE ATTENTION OF: Robin Keeler, DGS Holdings – Production Dept.
>
> **MESSAGE**
>
> I am sorry to report that the order dated May 22 for a consignment of part numbers DR 56821 and TR 55901 has been delayed due to production problems. We cannot ship the parts on June 10 as requested. Delay by three weeks, to July 1.
>
> We regret the inconvenience this may cause.
>
> Best regards,
>
> *Maria Pinto   Luis Deias*
>
> Maria Pinto and Luis Deias

You are very concerned about this. Contact your Portuguese subsidiary to find out the reason.

YOU:

- know that delays like this can affect production schedules for the whole organization

- have received five similar faxes in recent months

- want to visit Portugal with top level colleagues to examine reasons for continuing problems

- may, as a compromise, insist on sending one individual from head office to help resolve problems at the Portuguese plant

- have heard that there is a strike on at the moment

- may have to stop using your Portuguese subsidiary as a supplier – but naturally you do not want to do this.

YOU START.

© Penguin Books 1996

(Knowing; sequencing; measuring and calculating)

A profit and loss account is a statement of income and expenditure for a business in a particular time period, normally one year. It shows trading performance in terms of what has been spent and what has been raised through sales and other revenue generating activities.

At the end of the financial year, a colleague from a sister company asks you for details of the profit and loss account for your company, which has interests in retailing, leisure and property.

Use the abbreviated profit and loss account below to answer his/her questions.

YEAR TO 31 MARCH 19—		*Previous year*
Trading surplus (before depreciation)	$8.0m	(9.5m)
Income from property	$2.5m	(4.6m)
Less: depreciation	$4.0m	(3.5m)
Pre-interest profits	$6.5m	(10.6m)
Less: interest payments	$2.5m	(3.4m)
Pre-tax profits	$4.0m	(7.2m)
Less: tax	$1.3m	(2.3m)
Available to shareholders	$2.7m	(4.9m)

YOU:

- **think the fall in profit is due to a crisis in the local economy**

- **believe the main factor was a fall in income from renting office space. A lot of property owned by the company is standing empty**

- **think next year will be worse – you do not expect a quick recovery in the property market**

- **know that interest payments are down because several long-term mortgages were redeemed in the previous year**

- **think the company has done well to show a profit in very difficult trading conditions**

- **know that all property companies are in the same situation – most other leisure and retailing companies have also suffered.**

YOUR PARTNER WILL START.

47 PROJECT MANAGEMENT

(Agreeing/disagreeing; judging; measuring and calculating)

Project management is an important business activity which involves putting plans into practice. It requires the coordination of various activities, each within a specified time frame.

You are project leader for a company that is planning to build a new £2m production site. You have produced an outline of the project proposal. You have a meeting with the senior member of your team, the assistant project leader. Ask him/her for comments and get approval for your outline schedule.

Week	Phase	Action
6–7	I	Setting objectives
		Establishing definitions
		Establishing specifications
8–9	II	Organization
		Deciding project leaders and teams
10	III	Cost estimating and budgeting
11	IV	Putting out to tender
12–15	V	Detailed discussions
16–18	VI	Deciding on allocation of work
		Meetings with tenderers
19	VII	Contracts
20–21	VIII	Planning and scheduling
22–24	IX	Construction I: Site preparation
25–28	X	Construction II: Foundations
29–34	XI	Construction III: Above-ground structure
35–38	XII	Finishing work

© Penguin Books 1996

YOU:

- have based this schedule on your experience of building a similar production site at a subsidiary in Australia

- are absolutely confident about the accuracy of the schedule: 16 weeks planning + 16 weeks construction = 32 weeks total

- will accept only minimal changes to the schedule

- are responsible to the production manager and the managing director only

- understand that the company requires the project to be finished as soon as possible

- naturally do not want to upset members of your team.

YOU START.

(Agreeing/disagreeing; judging)

Quality improvement is the process of improving all the systems and procedures within your organization so that you produce better goods or services for your customers. Quality is not an absolute. The quality of your goods and services is defined by what your customers expect.

Your company has asked you and your partner to draw up a list of proposals for improving quality within your organization(s).

Select six of the following which you both feel should definitely form part of your company's new commitment to total quality:

- appointment of quality control inspectors for random checks on finished goods ☐
- creation of quality circles throughout the company ☐
- establishment of a regular quality competition with prizes for best suggestions for improving quality and saving money ☐
- introduction of a regular quality feature in the in-house magazine ☐
- decision to seek international quality standard (e.g. ISO 9000) ☐
- drafting of a quality charter to be sent to all customers ☐
- creation of telephone hotlines so that customers can get immediate help with problems and give immediate feedback on your products/services ☐
- introduction of a quality improvement training programme for all staff members ☐
- appointment of a top manager to have overall responsibility for the quality improvement programme ☐
- the establishment of quality targets (zero defects) in production ☐
- the prominent display of quality notices throughout the company buildings. ☐

Is there anything else you might like to add?

YOUR PARTNER WILL START.

© Penguin Books 1996

Quizzes are usually fairly light-hearted but they can also tell us quite interesting things about ourselves and about other people.

Ask your partner the following business quiz questions and then get him/her to ask you. You can either answer each question in turn or each of you can go through the whole list in turn.

1 Do you work mainly:
   a) for money?
   b) for power?
   c) for fame?
   d) for self esteem?

2 If you won a lot of money, would you:
   a) invest it in your company?
   b) start your own company?
   c) retire?
   d) spend it?

3 If someone asked you how much you earned, would you:
   a) tell them the right figure?
   b) tell them the wrong figure?
   c) ask them to reply to the same question first?
   d) refuse to tell them?

4 Which is most important for you in your work:
   a) chances to meet people?
   b) friendly colleagues?
   c) a sympathetic boss?
   d) a good physical working environment?

5 If you found your new boss very difficult, would you:
   a) try to discuss the problem with him/her?
   b) try to tolerate the situation?
   c) ask for a transfer to another department?
   d) leave the company?

6 In meetings, do you normally:
   a) say less than the others?
   b) say more than the others?
   c) say as much as the others?
   d) chair the meeting?

7 In your opinion, should the average business meeting last:
   a) no more than an hour?
   b) no more than an hour and a half?
   c) no more than two hours?
   d) as long as it takes to complete the business properly?

8 Do people in your company normally arrive at a meeting:
   a) before or on time?
   b) less than five minutes late?
   c) between five and ten minutes late?
   d) more than ten minutes late?

9 Which of the following would most increase your own productivity at work:
   a) more autonomy?
   b) more time?
   c) more computers?
   d) more money?

YOU START.

50 QUIZ 2

Student A

(Questioning)

Ask your partner the following business quiz questions and then get him/her to ask you. You can either answer each question in turn or each of you can go through the whole list in turn.

1 Do you socialize with colleagues outside work time:
   a) often?
   b) sometimes?
   c) occasionally?
   d) never?

2 If your boss told you that you were wanted to represent your company on a stand at a trade fair for five days, would the prospect:
   a) excite you?
   b) horrify you?
   c) frighten the life out of you? or
   d) would you ask for extra money?

3 Which is most important to you in your work:
   a) your telephone?
   b) your computer?
   c) your fax machine?
   d) your desk?

4 In your opinion, should your company be:
   a) research-driven?
   b) product-driven?
   c) market-driven?
   d) customer-driven?

5 How many days' holiday (including public holidays) do you think people should take off work per year:
   a) fewer than 15?
   b) between 16 and 25?
   c) between 26 and 35?
   d) more than 35?

6 How much time do you normally take for lunch at work:
   a) less than 30 minutes?
   b) 30–60 minutes?
   c) 60–90 minutes?
   d) more than 90 minutes?

7 Do you think an employee should be sacked if caught in the workplace:
   a) stealing?
   b) smoking in a no-smoking area?
   c) taking drugs?
   d) sexually harassing a colleague?
      (You may wish to choose more than one.)

8 Do you prefer to be paid:
   a) a high base salary with no fringe benefits and no performance-related bonus?
   b) a low base salary with good fringe benefits?
   c) a low base salary with performance-related bonus?
   d) a low base salary with performance-related bonus and fringe benefits?

9 Do you prefer to work:
   a) mostly in an office?
   b) mostly at home?
   c) mostly travelling around?
   d) a mixture of working at the office, at home, and travelling around?

YOU START.

© Penguin Books 1996

51 RAISING FINANCE

(Questioning; forecasting)

Companies can raise extra finance to help meet their needs in several ways. Three examples are by a flotation (the sale of shares), a rights issue (selling shares at a special low price to existing shareholders), or taking out a loan from a bank through a mortgage or debenture.

You represent Chapman Whitney Ltd. The company needs to invest in new plant to meet expansion plans. You arrange a meeting with your company's financial adviser to discuss your plans to raise extra finance.

Ask your adviser for his/her opinion on the expansion plans, and on the potential for raising extra money to support the plans, either through a flotation, or through a rights issue, or through loans from a bank or other lending institution.

Here is a part of the company balance sheet for the last financial year.

SOURCES OF FINANCE		$m
Share capital 4 million shares at $1.0		4.0
Retained profits		8.0
Shareholders' funds		12.0
Debt finance		
6% mortgage (3 years)	6.0	
Bank overdraft	4.0	10.0
Total funds		**22.0**
Assets employed		
Fixed assets		
Property	10.0	
Machinery	2.0	
Vehicles	2.0	14.0
Net current assets		8.0
Total assets		**22.0**

Fig. 1 Chapman Whitney Ltd. Abbreviated balance sheet.

YOU:

- admit that the company is not trading dynamically at the present time – sales are static in a contracting world market

- believe that you have the expertise to build new and innovative products for the next 25 years.

YOU START.

52 RECRUITMENT

(Liking and preferring; urging; declining/rejecting)

Recruitment is the process of looking for and finding people to do particular jobs. Recruitment can be a time-consuming and costly process. Recruiting the wrong person can be a very expensive mistake.

You are an American up-market designer of men's clothes, running your own medium-sized company jointly with your American partner. You provide the creative inspiration and your partner looks after the business side of things. You have a good working relationship. Your company has traditionally operated in the US and is now trying to break into the European market. You are based in New York and your partner has been in Paris for three months. You are phoning each other (at 10.00 French time, 17.00 US time) to decide which candidate should get the new job of sales and marketing manager for France (and potentially for the whole of Europe). Each of you has shortlisted two candidates whom you have personally interviewed. Unfortunately your fax machine is not working, so you have to describe your own shortlisted candidates to your partner over the phone.

1 **Read the two profiles below and decide which of your own two candidates you prefer.**
2 **Describe them both to your partner.**
3 **State your own recommendation.**
4 **Persuade your partner of the advantages of your preferred candidate.**

YOU:

• **strongly favour an American choice because you feel that an American will integrate much more quickly and easily into the company team and into the company's culture.**

Name	Jerome McGraw
Age	27
Nationality	American
Marital status	Single
Education	BA Business Administration, MBA Hartford
Experience	Marketing posts with Apple Computers and Coca-Cola (4 years total). Excellent references
Languages	Native English, intermediate Spanish, a little French
Salary expectation	Very reasonable: would go to Paris 'for peanuts'
Interests	All sports: captained championship-winning university basketball team; politics; clothes
Other relevant information	Comes from poor working class background; of African-American origin; well-balanced, very attractive personality, intelligent, ambitious; he obviously has enormous potential for progress up to senior management level; wants to make big impact on smaller company; desperately wants international experience

© Penguin Books 1996

Name	Nancy Guscott
Age	40
Nationality	American
Marital status	Divorced (3 years ago)
Education	MA (and PhD incomplete) in French language and literature
Experience	15 years' marketing posts in the US and Europe, specializing increasingly in up-market women's fashion: clothes and accessories – very good contacts in this sector. Currently Marketing Director for a reputable US mail order clothes company: $300m turnover per year. Some spin-off knowledge of men's fashion market
Languages	Native English, fluent Hebrew, fluent spoken French, good written French, some Italian
Salary expectation	Reasonable
Interests	Fashion, food, antique furniture
Other relevant information	A top-flight marketer of women's clothes. Vivacious, Francophile, spent several years in Paris with her French (now ex-) husband who has custody of their three children

YOU START.

53 RECYCLING

(Agreeing/disagreeing; judging)

Recycling is the activity of sorting out waste material so that it can be reprocessed by specialist companies. Recycling is broadly considered to be a sensible way to reduce the exploitation of the environment.

Your company produces 25,000 tons of waste products from its offices and canteen areas every year. At present there is no policy on recycling and you think there should be one.

Together with a colleague, decide on the three most important advantages of recycling and whether there are any important disadvantages. Then decide if you want to recommend the formal introduction of procedures on recycling and any related considerations.

YOU:

- **think the introduction of systematic recycling will finally bring the company into line with government recommendations**
- **think recycling is a 'good thing' and gives a good impression to everyone in the company**
- **fear that more space will be required for containers for different materials**
- **think employees will have to waste time sorting out different materials for recycling, i.e. paper, cardboard, metal, glass**
- **think that the company could save money by encouraging greater reuse of paper – especially for rough working, notes and internal messages**
- **think the company should use more double-sided printing and copying and so save paper.**

YOU START.

 © Penguin Books 1996

(Judging; negotiating)

Relocation means moving your home, office or factory from one place to another.

You are a manager with a European company which has recently entered into a joint venture agreement whose head office will be in Brussels. You have been offered a fantastic job by the new boss in Brussels. But your wife/husband and teenage children are very settled where they are and you don't want to move.

You therefore propose to commute from your home to Brussels on a weekly basis, travelling out every Monday morning and back every Friday evening.

YOU:

- **think you will be more productive away from your family and will not have the extra worry of their adjusting to a different environment**

- **will save the company a lot of money in relocation costs**

- **will, if necessary, give up your company car in Brussels to pay for the cost of the weekly return plane fare (you already have a company car at home).**

Discuss the question with your new boss at a meeting. You must reach an agreement. Although you want the job, you will not sacrifice your family's interests to keep it.

YOUR PARTNER WILL START.

© Penguin Books 1996

55 SALES TARGETS

(Measuring and calculating; correcting)

When you fix sales targets, you predict the quantity of goods or services you will sell during a future time period.

Your company's sales operation is divided into a number of regions, and you and your partner have joint responsibility for the Central region: you manage the West Central area and your partner manages the East Central area.

Last year the company's management announced a new incentive scheme for sales staff: the winning sales team would win a week's holiday in the Caribbean for themselves and their spouses. Although you made big efforts to sell more than the other regions, you saw the other teams pulling ahead of you. In addition, computer problems made you late with the figures for the last quarter of the year.

Your computer manager now tells you that some of the original figures for your area are wrong: the new figures are on the whole higher than you thought.

1 **Calculate your new total sales for the year.**

2 **Call your opposite number in East Central and see if, together, your figures are now good enough to win the prize.**

Figures in $US	North	West	South	East
First quarter	93,137	94,005	85,211	93,140
Second quarter	101,104	98,276	85,439	99,505
Third quarter	103,721	99,422	87,624	102,099
Fourth quarter	95,106	100,471		
Total				

Figures in $US	West Central Initial	West Central Revised	East Central Initial	East Central Revised	Central Revised Total
First quarter	46,010	46,910	47,194		
Second quarter	48,763	48,963	51,309		
Third quarter	49,345	49,727	51,499		
Fourth quarter	49,557	50,847	51,446		
Total					

YOU START.

© Penguin Books 1996

**(Welcoming; greetings and farewells;
introducing self)**

Small talk is a vital skill in business. It can be difficult to initiate a conversation and then to keep it going, but it is very important to be able to do so – in English as well as in your own language.

1   A visitor to your company is waiting to see your CEO (chief executive officer) and you have been asked to look after him/her for ten minutes. It is your job to keep the conversation going.

Spend ten minutes talking to the visitor. While you are talking, try to direct the conversation so that the visitor uses as many of the words below as possible. At the end of ten minutes, count up how many of the words in the box below he/she used.

> THINK / TRIP / MOUNTAIN / PHOTO(GRAPH)
> PORTABLE / EAT / COUNTRY/ FAST / HOLD / GREEN

YOU START.

2   When you have finished, repeat the activity. This time you take the role of visitor.

YOUR PARTNER WILL START.

© Penguin Books 1996

(Introducing self; questioning; expressing amazement)

Fill in the form below to invent a new indentity for yourself!

Name: ....

Nationality: ....

Age: ....

Address: ....

Company: ....

Company activity: ....

Position: ....

Responsibilities: ....

Length of service: ....

Current trip to: ....

Reason: ....

Family: ....

Interests: ....

Other information: ....

Now imagine that the 'new you' is sitting in a plane next to another business traveller and that you begin to talk. Tell the other person (your partner) as much as possible about yourself. And find out as much as possible about your partner.

YOU START.

© Penguin Books 1996

58 SPARE PARTS

Student A

(Obliging; regretting; measuring and calculating)

Parts, or components, are put together in manufacturing or assembly processes to make products, or are used to replace faulty or damaged parts in existing products.

Your company needs a special delivery of some parts to meet your production target for next month. You contact a supplier and ask for the following products. Your preferred delivery times are stated.

Part number	Quantity required	When required
FR4001	220	immediate delivery
FR4002	250	immediate delivery
GA20	140	7 days
GA25	100	7 days
HK287	250	7 days
HK320	250	14 days
HT10	750	14 days
XT10	100	14 days

YOU:

- prefer not to have any early deliveries as you operate a just-in-time production system
- cannot tolerate any delays in meeting your fourteen-day requirements
- could accept one or two days' delay on up to 50% of the GA components
- know that you are a very important customer for this supplier
- expect to pay on your usual terms: 60 days from delivery with 10% discount
- consider this order to be vitally important
- do have an alternative supplier, but the quality is slightly lower
- prefer not to use the alternative supplier, but you would if there was any risk of not getting the goods you need.

YOU START.

59 TEAM BUILDING

(Liking and preferring; judging)

More and more work is project work and more and more project work is done in teams. In the future, you could be a member of several teams working on several different projects at the same time. Team members play different but equally important roles and a good team is one with a good balance between roles.

You and your partner are forming a special team to work on a major new project. You are looking for two other people to join you to form a dynamic and balanced team.

Look at the brief descriptions of team roles below. A well-balanced team will have people with different preferences situated in different places on the wheel.

Reporter-Advisers gain information before taking action; interpret situations and give advice.

Creator-Innovators find new ideas and approaches; research; explore the future.

Explorer-Promoters look for new opportunities; find new contacts and resources; promote and sell ideas.

Assessor-Developers make ideas work in practice; develop prototypes and test plans.

Thruster-Organizers make things happen; organize what has to be done; ensure objectives are met.

Concluder-Producers carry things through; work to orderly plans and systems; meet deadlines.

Controller-Inspectors control processes; inspect standards; ensure procedures are followed.

Upholder-Maintainers clarify purpose, values and principles; provide support; maintain standards.

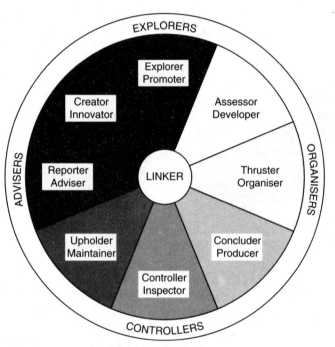

Margerison-McCann
TEAM MANAGEMENT WHEEL

The Team Management Wheel and role descriptions were developed by Charles Margerison and Dick McCann of Team Management Systems UK Ltd.

The Margerison-McCann Team Management Wheel is a registered trade mark of Prado Systems Ltd. For precise pinpointing of a person's preferred role, it is necessary to complete the Team Management Index, a questionnaire developed by Margerison and McCann, which also provides a detailed personal profile for reference during discussions aimed at improving teamwork.

Discuss with your partner:

- **which role you think you would prefer to play in the team**
- **which role your partner would prefer to play**
- **which other two roles you need to make a balanced team.**

YOU START.

     © Penguin Books 1996

(Blaming; agreeing/disagreeing; urging)

Managing your time well is one of the most important skills that anyone in business can learn. If you do not, the results are frustration for yourself and your colleagues, and loss of money for your company.

Below you can see several common problems for anyone who works in an office. Tell your partner about each problem in turn and see what solution he or she recommends.

The problems

1 My phone never stops ringing.
2 People are always coming in and out of my office.
3 I spend far too much time in meetings.
4 I can manage my time perfectly well. It's technical breakdowns and constant problems with computers which make it difficult for me to manage my time.

Now your partner is going to tell you about some other typical time management problems. Choose from the list of suggestions below the solution which you think is best for each problem and tell your partner about it. Add your own comments.

The solutions

a Prioritize. Delegate. Block time for important tasks. Keep things in proportion. If the problem persists, discuss it with a superior.
b Don't be afraid to tell people you're too busy right now. Stand up when someone comes in and don't sit down again if you don't want them to stay.
c Don't always agree to see people straight away when they ask to talk to you. Plan your day so that everyone knows that there is a time when you need to work alone and a time when you are happy to see other people.
d Never handle a piece of paper more than once. Either act on it, pass it on or put it in the bin.

YOU START.

© Penguin Books 1996

(Knowing; agreeing/disagreeing; sequencing)

Prioritizing is deciding on an order of importance for a number of possible actions, by comparing their usefulness. The most useful are often urgently required, while the least useful may be disregarded.

Your company produces high quality audio equipment for use by professional sound engineers in the music, film and television industries. You are planning a major sales and marketing drive in several new export markets in Europe and Asia. Your colleague is the new marketing director with responsibility for this major initiative.

Together with the marketing director, set priorities for training a staff of five marketing managers and 20 sales representatives and agents.

Decide on an order of one to nine; eliminating the lowest three or four areas of training – depending on your assessment of their value.

- foreign language training for reps and agents in the countries concerned
- foreign language training for your five marketing managers
- training in cultural awareness for five marketing managers
- training in developing new markets and marketing strategy for you as marketing director
- training in marketing strategy for reps and agents
- training in new product technology and after-sales service for reps and agents
- training in new product technology and after-sales service for marketing managers
- training in new support software for marketing campaigns for marketing managers
- production of detailed guidelines for sales reps and agents in various languages.

YOU START.

   © Penguin Books 1996

(Judging; agreeing/disagreeing)

Distribution is concerned with moving goods from the producer to the customer.

Your company wants to export goods from Spain to Greece. You have asked a colleague in Spain to suggest the most appropriate way of moving 120 tons of goods to Greece every month. In the meantime, another colleague in Greece has sent you a proposal, details of which are shown below.

FAX MESSAGE
From fax number: (30) 31 547699
To fax number: (33) 1-44567321

TO: ARANT Cie (Paris)   For the Attention of Export Dept.

Re. Transport of goods to Greece

Herewith cost proposal from Barcelona to Greece.

I suggest Andropolis S.A. of Thessaloniki – road hauliers. Road transport is better as more flexible. We can get goods moved around more quickly. Also easy distribution to Athens and Thessaloniki by same lorries.

Estimated costs:
Barcelona – Athens.
1×5 ton container @ $1,000 each
6 containers per 30 ton capacity lorry = $6,000.
Total four lorries per month = $24,000.
Cost reduction of 10% per lorry for every 10 hour delay if caused by accident to lorry or mechanical failure.

Additional lorries can be arranged.
All documentation taken care of by Andropolis.
Normal route: Barcelona – Marseille – Milan – Bari – transfer by ship to Greece – onward to Thessaloniki or Athens.
Time: five days.
Alternative route: overland takes 7 days and costs $1,000 dollars per load. Not recommended – subject to delays.

Compare the two proposals and decide which is more convenient.

YOU:

- **want to move the goods as economically as possible**
- **think the company can be flexible on delivery times – any time in the first week of the month is okay**
- **need flexibility – variations in the consignments must be possible.**

YOUR PARTNER WILL START.

© Penguin Books 1996

(Negotiating; measuring and calculating; forecasting)

The working environment has long been recognized as a key factor in improving productivity, employee satisfaction and in reducing days lost through sickness.

You are a manager responsible for the telesales office in a company with a turnover of £1.25m. You have a meeting with an employees' representative to discuss possible ways of improving the working environment for your team of eight people.

YOU:

- **believe that productivity will increase if significant improvements are introduced**
- **need to decide on various improvements within an overall budget limit of £16,000. This spending limit is confidential**
- **have received a memo from a management colleague showing the following cost estimates. These costs are also confidential.**

MEMO

CONFIDENTIAL

To: D-office
From: HT
Re: Office improvements

Redecoration	£4,500
Improved sound proofing between desk areas	£2,200
New triple-glazed windows	£3,800
Improved workstations, hands-free telephones, screens, footrests, etc.	£4,850
Replacement of neon strip lighting	£3,600
New ergonomically designed desks	£4,400
More office space	£15,000
New ventilation system	£5,200
New chairs	£1,000

Call if you want to discuss.

HT

YOU START.

 © Penguin Books 1996

(Regretting; declining/rejecting; agreeing/disagreeing)

Holiday entitlement is established in employees' contracts but the exact time when holidays are taken is usually negotiated between the company and the individuals concerned. The company naturally has to make sure that there is sufficient cover when employees are away on holiday.

You are responsible for the implementation of production schedules and work rotas in a fresh food factory. Here is a chart showing production schedules for July and August and work rotas for your two line supervisors, LS1 and LS2. The production capacity is 7,000 units per week, but this volume of production requires both line supervisors to be available for work as an additional smaller line has to be operated.

	week	M	T	W	T	F	S/S
JULY	27 4,500	4 SV: LS1/	5 LS2	6	7	8	9/10
	28 5,000	11 SV: LS1/	12 LS2	13	14	15	16/17
	29 7,000	18 SV: LS2	19	20 LS1– Va	21 cation	22	23/24
	30 7,000	25 SV: LS2	26	27 LS1– Va	28 cation	29	30/31
AUGUST	31 6,000	1 SV: LS1/	2 LS2	3	4	5	6/7
	32 5,500	8 SV: LS1/	9 LS2	10	11	12	13/14
	33 5,000	15 SV: LS1	16	17 LS2– Va	18 cation	19	20/21
	34 4,500	22 SV: LS1	23	24 LS2– Va	25 cation	26	27/28
	35 6,000	29 SV: LS1/	30 LS2	31	1	2	3/4
SEPTEMBER	36 6,000	5 SV: LS1/	6 LS2	7	8	9	10/11

In March one of your line supervisors (LS1) requested holidays in weeks 29 and 30. You provisionally agreed. Try to persuade him/her to have holidays at a different time.

YOU:

- **know that all production has to be for immediate delivery as the company makes fresh foods**
- **realize you have made a mistake and that the supervisor will have to be compensated**
- **know that the orders for July are from your most important customers.**

YOU START.

© Penguin Books 1996

65 WORKS COUNCIL

(Urging; agreeing/disagreeing; hesitating)

Many companies in the industrialized world have works councils: committees of representatives of both management and staff which meet regularly. However, the powers of works councils can vary widely from country to country and from company to company. In Germany and Scandinavia, for example, employees' representatives may participate in decisions about the company's financial, marketing and human resources strategy. Elsewhere, the works council may have a much more limited role.

You and your partner serve on the works council of the medium-sized company where you both work. The company employs 100 people. Each year the council is given a £5,000 Christmas present by the company's owners to spend in whatever way it wishes. You and your partner are meeting to brainstorm your ideas before the full council meeting to discuss the subject. You have jotted the following ideas down on the back of an envelope. Compare your notes with your partner's and try to reach a joint decision on what you would like to recommend. (You can add your own ideas to the list below.)

YOU think the money could go on:

- a Christmas party for the children of all staff: food, guest entertainer, and a present for each child

- a £50 cash gift per employee

- the donation of the entire sum to the company's sports association. The company soccer club's changing rooms badly need refurbishing

- a contribution to the company's TAA (Third Age Association) which would like to organize a home visiting service for elderly ex-staff members

- your own ideas.

YOUR PARTNER WILL START.

 © Penguin Books 1996

Student B

Material for photocopying

(Introducing self and others; questioning)

Ice breakers are short activities which help people get to know each other at the beginning of a training course.

Get the following information about your partner. One of you can ask all the questions first or you can take it in turns to ask each question.

---

1 Professional

Find out your partner's:

- name
- company
- company's activity (in one sentence)
- job title
- department
- job responsibilities (in one sentence)
- office location.

---

2 Personal

Find out about your partner's:

- home
- family
- journey to work
- leisure time activities
- favourite holiday location
- favourite restaurant.

YOUR PARTNER WILL START.

2 ADVERTISING

(Measuring and calculating; negotiating; urging)

Advertising is one aspect of promotional activity used by companies to increase consumer awareness of the company and its products, and to improve sales performance.

You work for an advertising agency. You specialize in the sportswear sector. You have received the following letter:

You prepare the following notes:

REGIS & BENNETT SPORTS COMPANY

9–10 Houchen Industrial Estate
Coventry CV3 2TH
Telephone 01203 542181 Fax 01203 542281

L. Barker,
Arrow Advertising Agency
114 Kings Road
LONDON SW3   16 May 19—

Dear Lee,

Following our recent meeting, I write to confirm that we look forward to hearing your suggestions for a new campaign to promote our Sporto range.

Please call to arrange a meeting to discuss your ideas.

Kind regards,

J Sillett

J. Sillett
Marketing Department

You prepare the following notes:

Advertise using
1. Sponsorship of athletes- Olympic Games - cheaper and more reliable than football sponsorship.
   → Cost estimate: £100,000
2. Advertising in sports magazines - targets serious sports activists.
   → Cost estimate: £5,000
3. TV advertising - expensive, but massive increase in consumer awareness.
   → Cost estimate: £200,000
4. Perimeter advertising in stadiums →
   Cost £20,000
5. Advertising on the street,
   → Cost: £25,000

No to football sponsorship - too expensive, male-orientated and too dependent on team success.

YOU:

- **cannot give any guarantee on increased sales but you can guarantee increased consumer awareness of the brand name, Sporto, if your client agrees to your suggestions**
- **have useful contacts with famous Olympic athletes – they are looking for sponsors**
- **cannot, of course, be sure that they will win gold medals**
- **accept that TV advertising is expensive – but it is the most effective**
- **would like your client to agree to spend more than £250,000 – perhaps up to £100,000 more.**

YOUR PARTNER WILL START.

 © Penguin Books 1996

3   AGENDAS

(Agreeing/disagreeing; judging)

An agenda consists of the points that will be discussed in a meeting, in order to reach agreed objectives. Not all meetings have written agendas, but everyone should understand the objectives of a meeting and know what issues will be discussed, within an agreed time.

Your company is planning a new quality programme. You are new to the company and you feel that communications within the company are not very good. You have received the following agenda.

Departmental Quality Development Group

Agenda for Meeting

Time: 9.30 – 11.00
Date: January 14, 19—.
Place: Head Office, Room 2–17.

1. Customer feedback
2. Internal suggestions
3. Quality standards

Comments welcome – Please call

Ring the project leader with your questions and/or suggestions for ways to improve the agenda.

YOU:

- **feel that the agenda is too vague – it should be more explicit. Make suggestions**
- **think the order of the three items is wrong – the question of standards is the most important so this should come first**
- **believe that communications within the company would be improved by having an internal quality newsletter**
- **insist that your suggestion is discussed in the meeting.**

YOU START.

4 BANK CHARGES

(Measuring and calculating; correcting; obliging; regretting)

Bank charges are the fees paid to banks for the various services they provide. Banks charge interest on the money they lend, but also charge fees for setting up loans and overdrafts, or for assisting in funds transfers, currency exchange, the provision of references, advice and a wide range of financial services.

You are a clerk for Credit Bank International. A small business customer calls with a query about a funds transfer that you have handled. Here is a copy of the notification of the funds transfer:

CREDIT BANK INTERNATIONAL

King's Cross Branch   Date: *24 June 19—.*

Please note that we have credited your account.

Your ref.   *Lee Pen & Co – China*

Invoice dated   *2 May 19—.*   Invoice total   *£2,020.00*

To   *F. Petersson S.A.*   Account number: *00878654*

AMOUNT   *£1,995.00p*

For Credit Bank International
HLT

Below is an extract from the agreement between the bank and the customer regarding international funds transfers.

---

16. International Funds Transfers
CBI will levy a standing charge of £10 on all international funds transfers. In addition, transfers from certain countries may be liable to an additional charge of 2% of the invoice total. Countries so affected include China, Iran, Iraq, Japan, North Korea, South Korea, Malaysia and several African states. Please contact the bank for the complete list.

YOU:

- **realize that the £25 deduction was wrong – it should have been £10**
- **realize that because the transfer was from China, the bank should have charged an extra 2% of the invoice total (£40.40)**
- **calculate that the customer should only have been credited with £2020 less £10 less £40.40 = £1,969.60p**
- **explain the mistakes to the customer and decide whether to debit the customer's account for a further £25.40p.**

YOUR PARTNER WILL START.

     © Penguin Books 1996

(Questioning; judging; hesitating; forecasting)

Budgeting involves combining sales forecasts with expected costs. Effective planning requires accurate budgeting and also a clear understanding of the effects of variations in any particular figure, from raw material costs to unit price or promotional costs.

Your partner presents a sales budget for an existing product, a mobile telephone called the CX20, to a finance meeting. He/she is proposing a unit price increase of 10%. He/she uses the following illustrations to show the effects of the price increase:

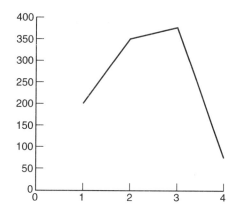

Fig. 1 Forecast sales over four quarters

| One: 200 | Two: 350 | Three: 375 | Four: 75 | Total = 1,000 |

Fig. 2 Unit sales forecast over four quarters

Estimated effect of 10% unit price increase

Unit price:	£150	£165
Sales:	£150,000	£160,875
Total cost of sales:	£50,000	£50,000
Cost of selling:	£78,000	£78,000
Total costs:	£128,000	£128,000
Gross profit:	**£22,000**	**£32,875**

Estimated effect of 10% unit price increase would be a 2.5% drop in sales.

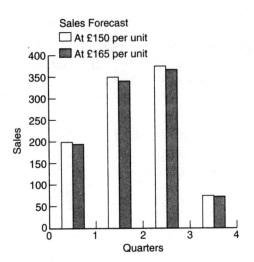

Fig. 3   Estimated effect of 10% unit price increase

| One: 195 | Two: 341 | Three: 367 | Four: 72 | Total = 975 |

YOU:

Discuss the price rise. Ask the following:

- **why is the cost of selling so high?**
- **how important do you think market share is?**
- **are there other ways to make the return on this product greater, instead of raising the price?**
- **how price sensitive is the market?**
- **are there ways to increase the price without losing sales?**
- **could sales be increased?**
- **what if competitors lowered their prices during the year?**

YOUR PARTNER WILL START.

© Penguin Books 1996

(Telling; sequencing; emphasizing)

An anecdote is a short story which you tell, usually about something which happened to you or to someone you know. Being able to tell a story is a very useful skill, both generally and in business: when talking to the person sitting next to you during a plane journey, for example. This activity gives you the chance to practise telling a story in a business context.

You and your partner are going to tell each other a story about a company. Your partner will begin the story and then, after two or three minutes, you will take over, using the first sentence below. Then your partner will take over again, then you will take over again, and so on. Try to talk for about one and a half minutes each time before handing over.

> 2 The big breakthrough came when . . .

> 4 Jo and Les began to have different
>   ideas about how the company should be
>   run . . .

> 6 Now Jo and Les are . . .

YOUR PARTNER WILL START.

© Penguin Books 1996

(Agreeing/disagreeing; questioning)

Business etiquette – forms of polite behaviour – can vary not just from one country to another, but also from one profession to another, from company to company, even from department to department. This exercise will help you measure how far you and your partner follow different codes of etiquette.

Your partner is going to tell you about five areas of office etiquette. In each case, your partner will first tell you how people behave in his or her company or department and will then ask you what the rules or conventions are in the company or department where you work. Discuss the differences.

Now do the same for the five areas below. First tell your partner how people behave in your company or department, then ask him or her about his or her workplace, then discuss the differences.

---

1 Business cards: do you present your business card to a new business contact:
- as soon as you meet?
- during your meeting?
- at the end of your meeting?

2 Kissing:
- is it ever socially acceptable to kiss work colleagues? If so, when?
- do you ever embrace or hug work colleagues?
- do women kiss other women more than they kiss men?
- do men ever kiss other men?

3 Socializing: do you meet colleagues outside the workplace:
- for lunch?
- for drinks after work?
- in the evening in your own home or in the home of a colleague?
- at the weekends?
- for music, cinema, theatre or some other sporting or cultural activity?

4 Hours: do people in your company tend to:
- start early and leave early?
- start late and leave late?
- start early and leave late?
- start late and leave early?
What is 'early'? What is 'late'?

5 Business at lunch: when lunching with business contacts, do you:
- talk business throughout the lunch?
- talk business only towards the end of the meal?
- talk business after the meal?
- not talk business at all?

YOUR PARTNER WILL START.

© Penguin Books 1996

8 BUSINESS GIFTS

(Agreeing/disagreeing; emphasizing; permitting; vetoing)

Business gifts are sometimes sent to customers or clients in the hope that they build goodwill – and help to secure business. In many cases the activity is perfectly reasonable and open – but in some cases the practice of offering and receiving gifts is connected to dubious behaviour, malpractice or illegal activities.

You are one of two purchasing directors in a large manufacturing company with a $70m turnover. One of your purchasers has been sent a case of Grand Cru Bordeaux wine by a supplier. Some of your management colleagues feel he should not have accepted this gift. At present the company has no policy on receiving gifts.

Together with your partner, decide on a new company policy on receiving gifts.

Prior to your meeting you draw up the following options:

MEMO

To:
From:
Date:

- Gifts policy-choices
- Any kind of gift should be accepted with a smile!
- If a new policy is adopted, all employees and suppliers should be told by letter.
- Only senior managers should accept gifts.

YOU:

- **personally like the idea of gifts – you have received some good ones in the past**

- **received a case of Grand Cru from the same company last year – but you didn't tell anyone**

- **think you and your colleagues would only judge suppliers on purely objective and factual considerations.**

YOU START.

BUSINESS INITIALS

(Knowing; correcting)

When reading the press in a foreign language, understanding the initials can sometimes create almost as many problems as understanding the words.

Here is a quiz to test and increase your knowledge of some basic – and not so basic – sets of initials which you could meet when reading the business press in English. First test your partner on what the following sets of initials stand for. Then your partner will give you a similar test. Then compare scores. Warning: each test gets harder as you go along!

1	**CEO**	(Chief Executive Officer)
2	**VIP**	(Very Important Person)
3	**HR**	(Human Resources)
4	**PR**	(Public Relations)
5	**PhD**	(Doctor of Philosophy)
6	**ECU**	(European Currency Unit)
7	**OECD**	(Organization for Economic Cooperation and Development)
8	**ABB**	(Asea Brown Boveri)
9	**JAL**	(Japan Airlines)
10	**DTP**	(Desk Top Publishing)
11	**CPU**	(Central Processing Unit)
12	**AOB**	(Any Other Business)
13	**GDP**	(Gross Domestic Product)
14	**USP**	(Unique Selling Proposition)
15	**TQA**	(Total Quality Assurance)
16	**IMF**	(International Monetary Fund)

YOU START.

    © Penguin Books 1996

10 BUYING AND SELLING

(Negotiating; urging; declining; rejecting)

Student B

Buying and selling a product or service, especially abroad, often involves negotiation – an agreement through discussion of the terms of the buying and selling arrangement.

You are the owner of a small company manufacturing computer games. You have just designed an exciting new game which you want to sell abroad. You have arranged a meeting with a potential agent (your partner), who operates in a region where there is a good market for new games. Using the table below, negotiate an agreement covering:

- **the number of units that the agent will agree to take**
- **the terms of payment: you are a small company and have the usual cashflow problems**
- **the discount on the standard price which you agree to pay the agent.**

Quantity	Terms	Discount
10,000 *Score: 5 points*	90 days *Score: 5 points*	30% *Score: 5 points*
20,000 *Score: 10 points*	60 days *Score: 10 points*	20% *Score: 10 points*
30,000 *Score: 15 points*	30 days *Score: 15 points*	15% *Score: 15 points*
40,000 *Score: 20 points*	Half in advance Half within 30 days *Score: 20 points*	10% *Score: 20 points*
50,000 *Score: 25 points*	In advance *Score: 25 points*	5% *Score: 25 points*

The agent may also ask you to provide:

- **a CD-Rom version of your software. The current version is on disk and is IBM-compatible, and, although you have begun the adaptation, you don't expect it to be ready for at least six months: score 15 points for delivery of a CD-Rom version in 6 months, 10 points for delivery in 4 months, 5 points for delivery in 2 months**

- **new packaging adapted to the local market: score 5 points if you resist**

- **promotional literature in the target language: score 5 points if you resist.**

Negotiate an agreement with the agent. Aim to get as many points as possible but do not reveal your scoring system to your partner. At the end of the negotiation, summarize your agreement under all six headings (quantity, terms, discount, adaptation, packaging and literature) and then compare your score with your partner's. Remember: your objective is to get as many points as possible but also to carry on doing business with your agent after the negotiation is finished.

YOU START.

11 CASHFLOW PROBLEMS

Student B

(Forecasting; judging; urging; negotiating)

Cashflow problems occur when a company has insufficient funds available to meet existing operating costs. A company may have full order books, but still suffer from funding problems while they wait for customers to pay.

You work in the marketing department of a company which has received an urgent order for 150 trailers from the government of a Gulf state. The trailers must be custom-built to meet highly specific requirements and must be delivered in only three months.

Your colleague is in the finance department and is not keen on the order because the present cash budget cannot accommodate it. Discuss the order and the present cash situation and decide what to do. Find out from your colleague:

- **how much cash is available**
- **the estimated cost of completing the order.**

YOU:

- **believe your company should accept the order – it could be a good lead-in to other business**
- **think that the existing cash budget should be redrafted to take into account income from the sale of a further 150 trailers – remind your colleague of this**
- **estimate that the order could add £700,000 to sales**
- **think your company should ask the bank for a short-term loan (about £250,000) to meet the costs of production**
- **think there would be no practical problem in meeting the order if support from the bank can be arranged quickly**
- **imagine that the customer would accept a tight payment schedule in exchange for a discount on the unit price – you can promise to negotiate this with the client**
- **think that a discount on the unit price would help secure the contract, if you can guarantee a three month delivery.**

YOU START.

© Penguin Books 1996

12 COMPANY OF THE YEAR

Student B

(Agreeing/disagreeing; emphasizing; judging; urging)

One way of encouraging small businesses to grow is to organize competitions with prizes for young companies with special entrepreneurial flair. A money prize can be very useful for a company with ambitions to expand but limited finance to do so. The only danger for competitors, successful and unsuccessful, is for them to spend more time on the competition than on doing business!

You and your partner together run a successful small business. You have just won a regional young business competition sponsored by the local press, television, local government and the local chamber of commerce.

First decide on the following:

Company activity: . . . .

Main markets: . . . .

Turnover: . . . .

Net profit margin: . . . .

Number of employees: . . . .

Now decide how you are going to spend the £100,000 first prize. Some suggestions are given below. Share your ideas with your partner and agree on a common plan. You should decide which options to go for and how much of the money to spend on each. Draw up a final investment plan for the whole sum of money.

YOU would like to:

- **expand the workforce (how many people? who?)**
- **establish an office in your main foreign market**
- **pay off the company's overdraft (£27,000)**
- **put the money into a special fund for eventually buying out your major local competitor**
- **organize a marketing trip to a part of the world which was previously too far and so too expensive to visit**
- **give a special bonus to all members of staff**
- **boost the training budget to provide all staff with increased training.**

List your own ideas.

YOUR PARTNER WILL START.

13 COMPANY ORGANIZATION

(Declining/rejecting; judging; liking and preferring)

Company organization is sometimes described in an organization chart or organigram, often a simplified diagram showing areas of responsibility for key personnel.

Your company, KEP Ltd, is involved in negotiations with a competitor, Altman Kopp, over a possible merger. In an informal meeting, you discuss ways to combine the two businesses into a single organization, allowing for the following facts:

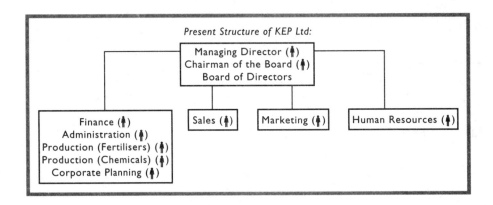

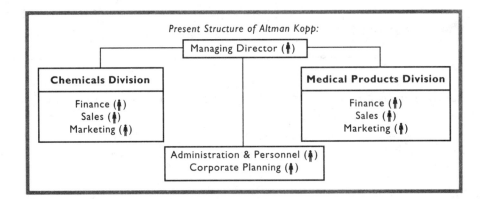

YOU:

- want to reduce your Board from eight to four members
- believe that your company should be a separate financial and cost centre
- already intend to merge Finance and Administration
- plan to abolish the Sales Department, incorporating it into Marketing
- for the purposes of the organization chart, you plan to merge your production activities, with everything under one director
- want to abolish Corporate Planning, bringing it under the Marketing Department.

YOUR PARTNER WILL START.

© Penguin Books 1996

(Questioning; sequencing)

Trade fairs are opportunities for individuals and companies to make contacts with potential customers and other professionals in the industry. While many companies hope to sign up orders for goods, most are happy to improve consumer awareness of the company and to promote the corporate image.

You are at a trade fair. You visit the stand of a company called Conta Inc. You talk to someone there about Conta. Ask in particular about:

- where the company is based
- overseas subsidiaries
- number of employees.

Interrupt to ask for clarification or additional information whenever you like.

Then talk about your own company, Edile S.p.A., using the following profile as a source of key facts.

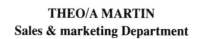

> **THEO/A MARTIN**
> **Sales & marketing Department**
>
> ---
>
> *Edile International (Singapore) Limited*
> *48 Tannery Row, Cencon Building,*
> *Singapore 1336*
> Tel 747 7676 Fax 747 7688

Name:	Edile S.p.A.
Sector:	Property development
Markets:	Italy, Europe, South East Asia, United States, Argentina.
199– Sales:	$373m.

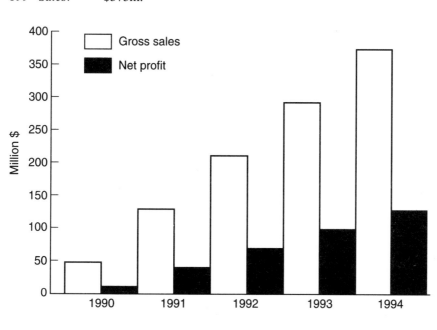

© Penguin Books 1996

Include any of the following additional information:

Head office:	Milan, Italy.
Subsidiaries:	Edile International in France, Germany, UK, Argentina, Singapore, United States of America (Chicago and New York) and (planned for next year) Brazil and Japan.
Worldwide employees:	more than 4,000.
Current major project:	new Space Research Centre in Houston, Texas.

Recent takeover of Bab Ltd (UK).

Note:
As an alternative, present your own company.

YOU START.

© Penguin Books 1996

(Greetings and farewells; sequencing; questioning, welcoming)

Showing a visitor round your company can be a useful way of winning customers as well as promoting the image of your company.

You are a potential client of a manufacturer of sweets and chocolates, a subsidiary of a major US food company. You are at the main plant of the company and one of its managers (your partner) is going to show you round the site.

Before you start, the manager is going to make a short presentation of the main features of the tour, using the plan below. He/she will tell you about the company's main products, its history and its organization. Then he/she will talk through the tour which you are about to make.

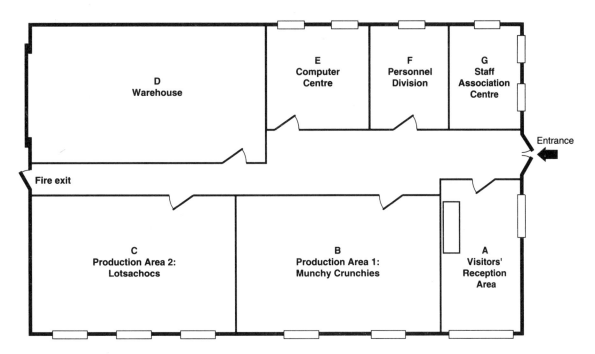

YOU:

are looking for a company which:

- **manufactures quality products**
- **is technologically sophisticated**
- **has progressive human resources policies.**

ask for as much detail as you can on:

- **the company's products**
- **its computer and telecommunications systems**
- **its health, safety and welfare policies**

while you listen to your partner's initial presentation.

YOUR PARTNER WILL START.

16 COMPANY VISIT

(Questioning; regretting)

Before you visit a company, it is useful to check with the person you are visiting about how to get in. Some companies, for example those involved in defence, can have strict security procedures which you need to know about in advance.

You are planning to visit a contact whom you met at a trade fair and who works in a large company which has recently tightened up its security because of industrial espionage. Your contact has faxed you a plan of the premises but the bottom half of the page of the fax was eaten by your machine. The meeting is tomorrow. Telephone your contact to ask how to get inside.

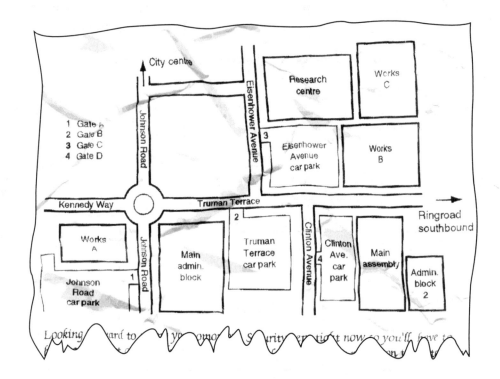

YOU:

- **explain that there was a problem with the fax**
- **find out where your contact's office is**
- **find out where to park**
- **find out which gate to use.**

YOU START.

  © Penguin Books 1996

17 CORPORATE CULTURE

Student B

(Agreeing/disagreeing; forecasting; hesitating)

The culture of a company is the set of beliefs, values, attitudes and organizational characteristics which make it unique. Some managers and business observers believe that changing the culture of an organization is the best way to significantly improve its business performance.

You and your partner woke up this morning to find yourselves joint heads of a large international company. Unfortunately, it is losing a lot of money. You both feel that a major transformation of the culture of the company is needed and you have brainstormed ten possible policies below. Now go through the list and decide together which ones you will implement.

---

1 You – the joint managing directors – should give up your big offices on the top floor and establish your base by the main photocopier on the ground floor.

2 Abolish individual pay, introduce pay based on team performance.

3 Aim for 50% of managers to be women within the next two years. (At the moment 60% of your employees and 5% of your senior managers are women.)

4 Abolish 'senior' management. Reduce the number of layers in the organization as far as possible.

5 Abolish the Personnel Department.

6 Make all managers fly economy class.

7 Abolish company cars. Pay people an allowance when they have to drive on company business.

8 Make all employees – yourselves included – wear a company uniform.

9 Make meetings shorter, have everyone stand up.

10 Instead of managers appraising subordinates, get subordinates to appraise managers.

You may come up with your own ideas as well.

YOUR PARTNER WILL START.

© Penguin Books 1996

119

18 CORPORATE SPONSORSHIP

(Forecasting; judging; urging; negotiating)

Corporate sponsorship is big business. Companies give money to sporting, cultural and charitable organizations as a way of bringing the company's name and products to the attention of a wider public.

Your company has decided to spend a large sum of money on some kind of sponsorship. You and your partner have been made responsible for recommending the best option to the Board. You have shortlisted three possible organizations you could sponsor. The cost of each option is approximately the same. You are now in a meeting with your partner to decide on the best option.

FILE 1

The football club in the city where your company is based has just lost its sponsor after going down from the national first to the second division at the end of the last season. Now the club is desperately looking for a replacement. The manager has been sacked and replaced by a well-known ex-international player with no previous managerial experience. There are no new players in the team. The club has large debts. Advanced sales of season tickets are poor and some people are saying that the number of spectators next season could be 20% down on last year. However, sponsorship would give your company excellent opportunities for advertising the company logo on the team shirt, in the weekly match programme and around the ground. You can expect two or three home matches to be televised live during the season. There are also good opportunities for corporate hospitality at home matches.

FILE 2

The government has reduced the grant it normally gives to your local city orchestra which as a result will have to disband if it is unable to find money from another source. In fact, you have already been approached by a committee of local art lovers, including some representatives from the city council, seeking your help. The orchestra currently does not have a permanent conductor. The average age of the players (who are employed on a part-time basis) is 49. The orchestra normally gives six to eight concerts per year, almost always in the Town Hall and another two or three during the city's annual cultural festival. One or two of these concerts might be broadcast on national radio each year. The orchestra has a regional rather than a national reputation but has traditionally been central to local cultural life. Some people say its programmes are too conservative: it rarely plays twentieth century music. Sponsorship would put your company name on concert programmes and on all promotional literature. You would have free tickets for all concerts to offer to clients and prospective customers.

  © Penguin Books 1996

FILE 3

Your city is the base for a young troupe of dancers who, in a short period of time, have gained a reputation for exciting choreography and innovative technique. One national newspaper critic hailed them as 'the most exciting development in modern ballet in the last twenty years.' The troupe is especially popular with young people: some of their most enthusiastic fans had never previously been to a performance of ballet. So far they have managed on a shoestring budget but are now receiving invitations to perform elsewhere in the country and even abroad, and they need money to invest in rehearsal rooms, to pay an administration manager, and so on. At the moment they have no permanent headquarters. The troupe are now actively looking for a sponsor and would be willing to incorporate the sponsor's name into their own name. Their activities are not, however, without controversy: there have been complaints about political bias in the themes presented in the dancing and some people have been shocked at what they see on the stage. You know that one of the Board members is unhappy about his teenage children attending their performances. On the other hand, you have been advised privately that the troupe could have an international reputation within the next ten years.

YOU START.

© Penguin Books 1996

19 COSTS AND REDUCING OVERHEADS

(Judging; emphasizing; forecasting)

Costs include production costs and the costs of selling. All aspects of a company's expenditure should be recorded as costs and good management aims to keep costs to a minimum within an agreed budget.

You work for a subsidiary of an international company. Your head office has sent instructions that costs should be reduced by 10% next year.

Discuss the following options with a colleague and decide which options you would introduce in order to meet the required savings.

- lay off 100 workers out of a total of 1,000 (5% saving)
- lay off 50 workers (2.5% saving)
- import more raw materials instead of buying from domestic suppliers (2% saving)
- use low energy lighting in non-essential areas of the plant (1% saving)
- reduce heating from 25°C to 22°C (2% saving)
- abandon plans to upgrade existing successful product range (3.5% saving)
- cut dividend to shareholders by 1% (2% saving)
- employ contractors to maintain equipment (2% saving).

YOU:

- **think the company can save money now before a major investment in new ventures in two years' time**

- **think your market share is very safe and that customer loyalty is high**

- **are sensitive to shareholders' opinions and wishes**

- **think that the company genuinely does need to reduce its workforce**

- **think using outside contractors could be useful for many (but not all) maintenance tasks**

- **think safety would not be affected**

- **realize you will have to compromise on some of these ideas.**

YOU START.

 © Penguin Books 1996

20 CUSTOMER CARE

Student B

(Questioning; judging)

Customer care is knowing your customers, knowing what they want, reacting to their changing needs, and keeping close to them. It is important for all members of business organizations to think about who their customers are and how they can improve their service to them.

You are part of a special task force set up by top management to improve customer care throughout the company. Your first job is to find out how customer-conscious your colleagues think the company is at the moment so that later on you can compare employee perceptions of customer attitudes with customer attitudes themselves.

YOU:

- explain the rating system below to a fellow employee (your partner), then

- ask the questions in the customer attitude survey below to find out how he/she thinks customers rate his/her company's current performance.

RATINGS:		
	Excellent	5
	Good	4
	Satisfactory	3
	Disappointing	2
	Unacceptable	1

How do you think your customers rate your company in terms of:

1 product quality ☐

2 after-sales service ☐

3 efficiency ☐

4 friendliness and courtesy ☐

5 frequency of contact ☐

6 understanding of customers' needs ☐

7 personalized service ☐

8 flexibility ☐

9 building long-term partnership, loyalty to customers ☐

10 anticipation of customers' future needs ☐

For any rating lower than excellent, what can your company do to improve the way customers see the company?

YOU START.

21 CUSTOMER COMPLAINT **Student B**

(Blaming; judging; negotiating; declining/rejecting)

When a customer complains, it is important to resolve the problem as quickly and courteously as possible.

You have just returned from a skiing holiday and have written the following letter of complaint to the company which organized the package.

> 23 Pennylong Avenue
> London NW2 5PG
>
> 27 February 199-
>
> Customer Relations Manager
> Super Skibreak Holidays
> 27 Porthill Road
> Oxford OX4 2AR
>
> Holiday receipt number FSB/403994/02/18
>
> Dear Sir/Madam,
>
> I have just returned from one of your so-called "February skiing breaks" extremely disappointed with your company's service for the following reasons.
> 1 The two-star hotel described in your brochure as a "comfortable family-run hotel" in fact offered only basic facilities and was dirty. The food was poor.
> 2 Your brochure also says that "if insufficient snow in your resort causes lifts and/or ski school to close, we'll do our best to arrange free coach transport to another resort where skiing is possible." Although skiing conditions were so poor on three days out of six that the skiing was unsafe, as your own local representative himself admitted, we were not provided with the transportation promised.
> The quality of this holiday was so bad that I feel that you should refund me the whole cost of the holiday. I should therefore be grateful if you would arrange for me to receive the sum of £691.40 as soon as possible. If I do not receive a satisfactory reply within seven days, I shall take legal advice.
>
> Yours faithfully
>
> *J. Cameron*
>
> J. Cameron

© Penguin Books 1996

YOU:

- are unhappy because you had really needed a break from a very stressful job and found the hotel and the skiing conditions below your expectations

- definitely felt that it was unsafe to ski at least half the time you were there

- would settle for less than you have claimed in your letter, but want Super Skibreak to offer significant compensation for the inconvenience you have been caused.

YOUR PARTNER WILL START.

22 CUSTOMS HOLDUP

(Questioning; urging; expressing amazement; regretting)

Frontier delays are usually caused by errors in the documentation accompanying goods. Occasionally other problems arise where the goods in a particular consignment do not match the description given to customs authorities.

You are a customs official at a frontier check. A lorry from Allen Deal Inc. has been stopped. The lorry is carrying electronic components and printed circuit boards. The driver has been arrested and is now in police custody. The lorry has been held for further examination of the cargo.

YOU:

- **discovered that the electronic components involved required an export licence and the driver did not have one**

- **intend to search the lorry to examine the cargo in detail in the next few days. You are very busy at the moment**

- **do not know where the driver is – the police have taken him away**

- **will not release the lorry until your boss says you can. This process sometimes takes several months**

- **cannot discuss the possibility of speeding up the release of the vehicle over the phone, although you could be willing to arrange a face-to-face meeting.**

YOUR PARTNER WILL START.

© Penguin Books 1996

23 EMPLOYEE MORALE

(Urging; sequencing; agreeing/disagreeing)

Many companies are reducing the size of the workforce, while at the same time expecting their employees to provide a high level of customer care. Maintaining the morale of the staff is both difficult and necessary, and is becoming more and more a central management challenge.

You and your partner, in the Human Resources department of a company which is in the process of reducing its workforce by 20%, meet to devise a strategy to ensure that employee morale remains as high as possible during the period of downsizing.

Tell your partner about the following list of five strategic actions which you have drawn up. Your partner will also tell you about the points which he or she has noted. Then, together, choose the five key actions for your strategy in order of priority.

YOU want to:

1 **introduce full consultation with the trade unions on future redundancies**

2 **introduce performance-related pay for all staff**

3 **promise training-for-all and training-for-life programmes for all staff**

4 **create career development plans for all staff involving full consultation with each individual staff member**

5 **increase funding for the Communications Department, in particular for the in-house magazine.**

YOU START.

© Penguin Books 1996   127

24 ENTERTAINING VISITORS

(Greetings and farewells; introducing self and others; questioning; welcoming; sequencing)

Corporate entertainment is often an important part of building good relations with business partners. Entertainment may be formal and highly planned, involving prominent people from the company or the region; in other cases, entertainment may be more personal and informal.

You are visiting a business partner for the first time. It is the first time you have gone to his/her home town.

Your partner telephones you to discuss a three day social programme, before you finally begin to talk about business.

YOU:

• **answer your partner's questions.**

YOUR PARTNER WILL START.

Some weeks later, you telephone your partner to invite him/her to your home town. Plan a single day's formal entertainment for your guest. Offer some top quality corporate entertainment, including a private concert by local musicians sponsored by your company.

Check that your guest is pleased with your ideas. Change any aspects of the programme that your partner is not happy about.

YOU START.

 © Penguin Books 1996

25 ENVIRONMENTALLY FRIENDLY OFFICE

(Sequencing; urging; agreeing/disagreeing)

More and more companies are becoming concerned about the effect their activities have on the natural environment. Some companies are carrying out environmental audits, others are publishing environmental accounts which try to measure this impact. There is no doubt that this will become a major activity of companies in the future.

As part of a campaign to make your company more environmentally friendly, you and your colleague have been made responsible for improving the environmental balance in the office block where you both work.

Look together at the following suggestions and prioritize them.

---

1 Separate waste bins for paper and plastics.

2 Separate waste bins for batteries (before recycling).

3 Separate waste bins for newspapers and magazines (before recycling).

4 Separate waste bins for glass (before recycling).

5 Use of recycled paper for the photocopier.

6 An indoor plant on every desk.

7 A daily record sheet for all photocopies made.

8 A daily photocopying quota per department to reduce by 25% the number of photocopies made.

9 A policy of turning off all electric lights in unoccupied rooms.

10 Punishment of employees who leave lights on in unoccupied rooms.

11 Use of low energy light bulbs throughout the building.

12 Reduction of the temperature by 5°C throughout the building.

13 Installation of double glazing throughout.

14 Incentives to encourage employees to travel to work by public transport rather than by car.

15 Any other suggestions which you and your partner can offer to make your offices more environmentally friendly places.

YOUR PARTNER WILL START.

26 EQUAL OPPORTUNITIES

(Agreeing/disagreeing; correcting; liking and preferring)

Equal opportunities is an area where many companies and many states have rules or legislation designed to protect specific groups from discrimination or unfair treatment. Such areas as terms of contract, wages and salaries, career prospects, job security and working conditions are affected by equal opportunities policies.

You are part of a discussion group which must produce recommendations to the Board on ways to improve the position of women in the company.

Note that:

- **58% of the 400 company employees are women**
- **only 5% of management positions are held by women**
- **the company has no policy on encouraging women to return to work after maternity leave, consequently only a very small number do return**
- **the Chairman has said he wants to improve the position of women in the company.**

In discussion with a colleague, prioritize the following suggestions (from the most important to the least important) to create an enlightened and progressive policy for employment.

- Actively encourage women to return to work after taking maternity leave.
- Improve internal training opportunities, encouraging women to apply for internal promotions.
- Encourage more part-time work, job-sharing, etc. with full employee rights.
- Introduce flexible time-tabling (flexitime).
- Provide crèche facilities.
- Improve maternity leave with full job security.
- Set a quota for female representation in management positions.
- Corporate statement on sexual harassment to be included in employment conditions.
- A promise from management to investigate reports of sexual harassment immediately.
- More liberal attitude towards women's choice of clothing.

YOU START.

© Penguin Books 1996

(Judging; knowing; hesitating; correcting; declining/rejecting)

Franchising is running a business which appears to be part of a chain of similar businesses, each with the same name, image and ethos, similar products and a similar marketing strategy. A franchisee pays a franchisor a fee and in return gets advice and support on how to run the business.

You are an area manager for a franchising company, Eet Up, which has over 300 fast food outlets. You have a meeting with the manager of one of them, in a medium-sized town. You need to sort out some problems.

You have received the following letter – you have added some points showing your thoughts. You realize you will have to compromise on some issues, but do not want to give much away.

```
A. Cook
Area Manager (Franchise Agreements)
Eet Up
Park Grove
London SW15 2RT                                22 November 19—

Dear Mr Cook,
Following  our  recent  conversation,  I  write  to  confirm  the
points for discussion at our meeting next month.  I would like
to talk about the following changes to our present agreement
which is due for renewal in the Spring of next year:
   - a reduction in the franchise fee from the present
     $50,000 per year.
```
At present size, no reduction possible.
```
   - a 50% grant towards the costs of developing the site.
```
How much extra seating? Grant possible. Then 5-10% less fee - depends on size.
```
   - freedom to buy ingredients locally.
```
Impossible! Brand identity and uniformity is essential!
```
   - Eet Up to run more on-site staff training.
```
Okay
```
   - preparation of a quarterly business report to Eet Up,
     not monthly.
```
No!
```
   - Eet Up to sponsor special promotions, such as
     combinations with theatres, cinemas, clubs, etc.
```
Possible
```
   - Eet Up to send more information on market trends.
```
O.K.
```
Looking forward to a successful meeting,

Best regards,

Steve Bailey
```

YOUR PARTNER WILL START.

28 HEALTH AND SAFETY

Student B

(Obliging; permitting; emphasizing; urging)

Companies are controlled by legislation affecting health and safety. In addition, many have their own policies to ensure that health and safety issues are constantly monitored and improved where necessary.

Your company has a very bad record on health and safety. Employee representatives and government officials have demanded immediate improvements; otherwise the company may be forced to close.

You have a meeting with a colleague to discuss ways to improve the situation.

The following is an extract from a report on incidents concerning health and safety in recent months.

```
January 12:     Casual worker electrocuted by faulty
                wiring.
February 15:    Fork lift accident - worker
                hospitalized. The operator was not
                qualified to use a fork lift.
February 17:    Worker falls off a roof while carrying
                out a repair.
April 4:        Chemical leak from a faulty waste pipe.
May 19:         Chemical leak: undiluted chlorine
                agents polluted nearby river.
July 2:         Roof blown off storage depot in a
                storm. Two workers injured.
August 23:      Fire on a rubbish tip.
September 2:    Night security man attacked by
                intruder. Not discovered for two hours.
                Received hospital treatment.
October 16:     Lorry crashes in despatch area.
                Witnesses say driver was going too
                fast. A lot of damage caused to
                vehicle: driver unhurt.
```

YOU:

- **basically agree that major improvements are necessary**
- **are not keen on spending a lot of money**
- **think casual labour and part-time labour is much cheaper than employing full-time, trained workers**
- **are prepared to make radical changes if there could be improvements in productivity which cover the increased costs**
- **are reluctant to make many short-term commitments on improvements in working conditions or training.**

YOU START.

 © Penguin Books 1996

29 IN-HOUSE MAGAZINE

(Agreeing/disagreeing; liking and preferring; measuring and calculating)

An in-house magazine can be an important tool for internal communication. It can serve to inform staff members of important company developments and encourage them to identify with corporate objectives.

You and your partner are members of a small task force formed to upgrade your company's in-house journal. You have been given a free hand to draw up a set of recommendations to submit to senior management.

You must:

- **identify the objectives of the magazine**

- **decide on how often the magazine should appear**

- **decide on the page size, number of pages and general look**

- **think of a name**

- **draw up a budget for a magazine with a circulation of 5,000 (editorial, design and production costs).**

For the content, decide which of the following you think should or should not appear in each issue:

- **a message from the Chairman of the company**

- **recent sales figures**

- **other financial information relating to the company's performance**

- **news and photographs of new recruits**

- **news and photographs of recent retirements**

- **features presenting individual employees**

- **features presenting the work of individual departments**

- **company sports news, social club news, news from the company's various clubs and associations**

- **interviews with senior executives**

- **trade union news**

- **a summary of coverage of the company and its products in the national and specialized press**

- **future plans for expanding or contracting the workforce**

- **recent acquisitions, joint venture agreements**

- **recent product launches, news of future product plans**

Can you think of anything else which should be included?

YOUR PARTNER WILL START.

30 INTERVIEW TECHNIQUES Student B

(Judging; agreeing/disagreeing)

Interviewing technique affects both the style of an interview and the type of questions asked. Many interviews use a combination of approaches to discover as much as possible about the applicant.

Look at the following job advertisement:

MARKETING MANAGER

An expanding young software development company with 950 employees, with its head office in London and with production sites in London, Rotterdam and Paris, is looking for a dynamic, ambitious graduate with experience in direct selling and strategic planning, preferably in a relevant sector.

Telephone 0800 5656 and ask for Freephone Professional for further details and an application form.

With your partner, classify the following interview questions into three groups: Personal/ Psychological (PP), Academic and Professional Background (AP), Hypothetical (H). Then assess them on a scale of 1 to 5: where 1 = most useful in a job interview, and 5 = not useful at all. Give reasons for your assessments.

1 Can you give an example of a situation where you have been in conflict with colleagues in your present job or in a previous job?
2 Do you enjoy working alone or do you prefer teamwork?
3 How does your experience until now prepare you for the work in this company?
4 How does your family feel about your relocation to London?
5 Given your lack of experience in software development – your background is in the food sector – is this likely to be a problem?
6 What do you do when you need to relax?
7 If a product you were responsible for was obviously failing in a particular market, what would you do to resolve the situation?
8 How do you see the future of the computing industry in ten years' time?
9 Can you describe a particular project that you have been closely involved with in your present job?

YOUR PARTNER WILL START.

 © Penguin Books 1996

(Questioning; urging)

A job application is a formal request for a job. You usually make an application by replying to an advertisement. People who apply for a job are job applicants.

You saw the following job advertisement in the newspaper five weeks ago and immediately sent your letter of application. Since then you have heard nothing apart from the acknowledgement below. Call the current personal assistant (your partner) to find out what has happened to your application. You also want to know more about the job:

- **travel: how much and where to?**
- **hours: typical working hours?**
- **pay: bonuses depend on what?**
- **what are the main problems?**
- **the name of the director!**
- **any other details you would like to have.**

And remember: this is the chance of a lifetime – sell yourself!

- **you speak your own language, English and one other language fluently**
- **you can type, and have good word processing experience**
- **you have a clean driving licence**
- **you are hard-working, flexible and have good communication skills**
- **you can start tomorrow.**

HELP! MY PA IS LEAVING ME!

In fact, we're parting on good terms after five years but I need a replacement FAST. If you've got what it takes to be PA to a well-known film director, write to Box XPA/475 at this newspaper now. Good salary (performance-related). No previous film industry experience required.

MEGA MEDIA ENTERTAINMENT

71 Gracechurch Street
London N1 1QA
Tel: 0171 222 7548 Fax: 0171 358 6037

Berlin – London – Paris – New York – Rome – San Francisco

Thank you for your recent application for the advertised post. You will hear from us very shortly.

Yours sincerely,

Linda Devito
Linda Devito

YOU START.

32 LARGE VERSUS SMALL COMPANIES

(Liking and preferring; judging; correcting)

A company's workforce may range in size from one employee to tens of thousands of people. Some people prefer to work in small companies, others prefer to be part of a large organization.

In this activity, you are going to debate with your partner the advantages of working for large and small companies. You prefer large companies, your partner prefers small. Use the arguments below to help you win the argument. Add your own arguments to the discussion.

YOU believe the following arguments:

1 In a big company, there are more people to meet. It's more stimulating.

2 In a big company, if you don't get on with one group of people, you can get a transfer to another department.

3 There's more opportunity for specialization in a big company. And there's more mobility within the organization.

4 People in big companies earn more money.

5 You feel proud of belonging to a company which has a national or even an international reputation.

6 People who work in big companies are not afraid of competing with large numbers of other able and talented people.

7 Big companies are stronger during downturns in business. You're less likely to lose your job because the company is less likely to go bust.

8 The advantages of working in a big company are more resources, bigger responsibilities, more opportunities.

9 You've got more chance of realizing your full potential in a big company.

You also think that . . .

YOU START.

 © Penguin Books 1996

(Urging; emphasizing; negotiating)

Cashflow considerations may sometimes create difficulties where naturally one company wants immediate payment but the other prefers to delay as long as possible.

It is now January 7th. You have not paid the following invoice for services received in November. The creditor calls to ask about your intentions regarding the payment.

KWAN SERVICES

450–58 Jalan Bukit Bintang
55100 Kuala Lumpur, Malaysia
Telephone (03) 77878779   Fax (03) 77878562

INVOICE

Arndale Promotions
112 Depot Row
PO Box 4567
Auckland, New Zealand

2 December 199–

Ref. Your order dated 24 September
Singapore Market Analysis Consultancy Report

Fee:	$US4,000
Expenses:	$US 567

TOTAL NOW DUE	$US4,567

Bank details:
KWAN Services Current account No. 70852406
Branch Sorting Code: 20-99-56
Credit Bank International,
Jelan Melaka 200, Kuala Lumpur, Malaysia.
Terms:
30 days from date of invoice.

YOU note that:

- **you have cashflow problems**
- **the report supplied by KWAN came two weeks later than they promised**
- **you have a policy of paying 60 days from invoice date (but sometimes you agree to pay before 60 days).**

YOUR PARTNER WILL START.

34 MANAGEMENT AND LEADERSHIP SKILLS FOR WOMEN

(Urging; negotiating; agreeing/disagreeing)

Companies and training organizations are increasingly offering courses especially for women, for example in leadership skills and assertiveness, in order to help women increase their self-confidence and their belief in their own ideas and actions in professional and personal situations.

You and your partner are helping with the design of a new training programme which will eventually be followed by all female employees who are managers or who have management potential, as part of the company's overall employee development programme.

You have identified five problem areas to look at during the course.

1 Dealing with a team member who is not pulling his or her weight.

2 Handling former colleagues who are jealous of your success.

3 Managing employees who are older than you.

4 Managing men.

5 Supervising a close friend.

Decide with your partner:

- **the best way to handle these problems**

- **a training idea (role play, simulation, game, discussion, case study . . .) to help the course participants to learn how to handle each situation better.**

YOU START.

  © Penguin Books 1996

35 MANAGEMENT QUALITIES

(Sequencing; judging; agreeing/disagreeing)

It is difficult to find universal agreement on the specific personality and professional characteristics which make a good manager. Team building usually aims to cover a range of qualities as one individual cannot have all the positive management attributes.

Discuss the following characteristics of what makes a good manager and, with your partner, rank them in order of importance:

- ability to get on well with colleagues ☐
- technical knowledge ☐
- experience of management in different industrial sectors ☐
- ability to make people laugh ☐
- willingness to work up to 60 hours a week ☐
- confidence in making decisions ☐
- concern for well-being of every employee from the top to the bottom of an organization ☐
- ability to understand details of company activity ☐
- ability to plan and understand corporate objectives ☐
- knowledge of the world ☐
- highly educated and cultured individual with wide range of personal interests ☐
- commitment to making money ☐
- stable health and psychological make-up ☐
- supportive family ☐
- ability to motivate ☐
- ability to delegate ☐

YOU START.

(Questioning; liking and preferring)

Companies sometimes employ external consultants to carry out market research to help them target products and services better. Some market research is very useful, but the techniques used to gather information have to be carefully designed.

You work for a marketing consultancy. A hotel chain with several hotels and restaurants has asked you to run a survey of customer opinions on the quality of service provided in their establishments. You carry out a survey using a questionnaire left in hotel rooms. After receiving more than 1,000 completed forms, you analyse results and send a preliminary report to the Marketing Manager of the hotel group. Here are the preliminary results:

PRELIMINARY REPORT

Number of respondents: 1,147

Survey technique: Customers staying in your hotels were asked to complete a form which was left in hotel rooms.

Analysis by purpose of visit:
Business: 78%   Private/tourism: 22%

Analysis by duration of visit:
One night: 48%   2 nights: 33%   3 nights: 10%   More than 3 nights: 9%

Analysis by services used:
Bed & Breakfast only: 65%   Evening meal: 35%

Quality Assessment:
1 = outstanding   2 = very good   3 = average   4 = poor   5 = very bad

Welcome on arrival:	2.5
Quality of service at reception:	2.1
Facilities available from reception:	3.0
Rooms, comfort, decor, etc.:	2.4
Beds:	3.0
Room service:	2.6
Value for money:	3.4
Breakfast:	2.8
Dinner/restaurant:	2.9

YOU:

- **see this research as only a first step and think more research is needed**
- **would like to conduct telephone interviews with hotel guests a week after their stay**
- **have the addresses and phone numbers of 825 of the respondents**
- **think that in your experience the scores should be around 2.0–2.5 to indicate a satisfactory level of performance**
- **do not have details on what percentage of the guests completed the forms but you think more than 50% did**
- **did not detect much difference in results between hotels in the group.**

YOUR PARTNER WILL START.

          © Penguin Books 1996

(Questioning; liking and preferring)

Market research is the activity of collecting information about consumers and what consumers want and need. This information is used to help produce the goods and services which will ensure success for the company.

You are walking along the street and are not in a great hurry. Someone is conducting a market survey. You agree to answer his/her questions.

YOU:

- **want to know who is asking you the questions and why they are asking, what company they represent, if the survey is anonymous and if you will receive any junk mail**

- **don't like giving information away for nothing**

- **don't like being asked anything personal.**

YOUR PARTNER WILL START.

38 MEETING ARRANGEMENTS Student B

(Obliging; declining/rejecting; urging; judging)

One definition of a meeting is: the gathering together of a group of people for a controlled discussion with a specific purpose. The essential elements of a meeting are:

- *a purpose: problem solving, idea-gathering or training*
- *an agenda: the list of points to be discussed*
- *the members: the chairperson, the secretary and the other members*
- *a result: the outcome of the process*
- *a report: usually the minutes (written by the secretary).*

You are an agent for electrical goods. A supplier from overseas calls about some products that you sell for him/her.

YOU:

- **accept that your sales performance has not been brilliant**

- **are very busy and have several more important and more successful products on your mind**

- **do not really want a meeting**

- **would prefer to discuss things by phone.**

Here are your appointments for next week:

13 Monday	16 Thursday
	Big Plan Group Meeting 8.30–5.30
14 Tuesday	**17 Friday**
Meeting with FRD – all day.	Meet Jo 8 p.m. Grand Hotel
15 Wednesday	**18 Saturday**
Call Alex 10.30 Meet Marie 8 p.m. Excelsior Hotel	**19 Sunday**

YOUR PARTNER WILL START.

© Penguin Books 1996

(Knowing; judging; urging; sequencing; permitting)

A mission statement is a statement of the aims, purpose and future activities of an organization. The objective of the mission statement is to define – for the company's employees, its customers and its shareholders – what kind of organization it is, what it believes in, and in which direction it wants to go.

You and your partner both work for the same international company. You have been given the job of producing an effective mission statement for your company. Your task is to draft a first version of the statement for circulation, about a dozen sentences long.

Your draft could include statements about:

- **the usefulness of the company's products and services in the community**

- **the company's objectives**

- **the company's values**

- **the company's policies on quality and on customer care**

- **the company's principles on personnel**

- **the company's policy on the environment and towards the countries of the developing world**

- **anything else you think is important.**

YOUR PARTNER WILL START.

(Negotiating; declining/rejecting; urging)

Most employees get some benefits from their employer in addition to their basic pay. Some senior managers receive very generous fringe benefits from their companies, which together are worth much more than the salary alone. Some people prefer to receive just money for the work they do; others prefer to receive pay plus other kinds of benefit. The total of what you receive is called your remuneration package.

In this exercise, you play the role of an executive talking to your partner who is a personnel manager in the company where you both work. Until now, the company has offered its more senior managers a wide range of benefits in addition to basic salary. Now, however, the company wants to cut the range of benefits being offered and wants to bring earnings under tighter control. Look at the information below and discuss with your partner how your remuneration package can be altered.

Current package per annum

Base salary	£20,000
Performance-related bonus last year	£10,650
(Note: maximum possible PRB was	£20,000)
Company car and private use of petrol	£3,600
Long-term disability cover	£1,500
Subsidized lunches	£1,250
Employer contributions to company pension fund	£1,200
Private medical insurance	£1,200
Parking	£950
Life assurance	£300
Annual health screening	£200
Financial planning	£200
Health club membership	£150
Total	**£41,200**

YOU:

- **want to increase the overall value of your new package**

- **are not very happy with the way the performance-related element of your pay is assessed and you do not want this part of the package to be more important than in the past**

- **appreciate and enjoy the range of fringe benefits you currently receive and do not want to lose too many of them. Some of them will be more expensive if you have to pay for them yourself.**

- **are aware that the company is currently reducing its workforce and several of your colleagues have recently been made redundant. So you do not want to appear to be too uncooperative.**

YOUR PARTNER WILL START.

    © Penguin Books 1996

(Emphasizing; blaming; telling; expressing your fear/worry; vetoing)

Evaluation and appraisal are used to ensure that employees develop their full potential within the company. Accurate assessment is vital in determining pay, career development and the company's commitment to individuals.

You are a manager in a production company. You have a meeting with a colleague to discuss an employee who is doing badly at work. Last week he failed to arrive on Monday and Tuesday, he was late on Thursday and on Friday he incorrectly completed work record forms.

Here is an internal report on the employee involved:

EMPLOYEE PERFORMANCE EVALUATION & HEALTH REPORT
STRICTLY CONFIDENTIAL

Name: John Casenove
Sex: M
Position: Line operator/Chargehand

History

John Casenove joined the company three years ago. For eighteen months his record was above average, with a good level of performance, low absenteeism and excellent inter-personal relations. He was promoted to chargehand 18 months ago.

For six months he responded well to the promotion and continued to be a valued employee.

Recent problems

Casenove began to arrive late for work and was frequently absent. A supervisor's report said he appeared depressed and uninterested. He was offered counselling by the company counselling service. The offer was refused.

Three months ago he was disciplined for assaulting a colleague. He was fined one week's wages.

He was warned as to his future conduct.

YOU:

- **feel the company should support an employee who used to be highly reliable**

- **do not think the company should sack Mr Casenove**

- **would prefer the following options:**
  a) offer him additional responsibilities
  b) persuade him to use the company counselling service
  c) warn him that indiscipline or continued absenteeism could cost him his job
  d) find out if he has seen his doctor.

YOU START.

(Sequencing; questioning)

Presenting information is a skill requiring clear organization and concise description. Keep your presentations simple, use short sentences and a clear structure.

Give a three-minute presentation on one of the topics below. You have two minutes to prepare your presentation. At the end your partner will ask you one or two questions.

Then ask your partner to present some information to you. Afterwards, you must ask one or two questions.

Repeat the task with another topic if you like.

Topics:

- **industry in your region**
- **something you bought recently**
- **tourism in your country**
- **changes in business**
- **a hobby you enjoy**
- **company organization**

YOU START.

                    © Penguin Books 1996

43 PRESS AND PUBLIC RELATIONS   Student B

(Judging; knowing; agreeing/disagreeing; vetoing)

Public relations is concerned with the image that society in general and customers in particular have of a company. All companies, especially larger ones, are very concerned to develop a good corporate image through their products, services, personnel, brand names and logos. The reputation of a company is formed through attention to all aspects of public relations. Bad publicity of any kind can have serious commercial consequences.

You are a journalist investigating a serious pollution incident at a chemicals factory. Chlorine and other bleaching agents leaked from a factory into the local river and killed hundreds of fish.

You are sent to interview a company representative. In your interview, find out what happened, when it happened, why it happened and what the company plans to do to stop any repetition.

The following briefing sheet will help you:

CHEMICAL POLLUTION TO RIVER

Company: KAD Ltd
Incident: 20 October

Background
- Local people have always been concerned about poor safety and environmental protection at the plant.
- Former employees have criticized safety.
- 45 pollution incidents in the past ten years.
- Fifteen years ago a gas leak caused panic in the area and the company was closed for six weeks.
- KAD spends too little on environmental protection.
- Safety and supervision at the plant during the weekend is practically non-existent.
- Leak detection systems are available.
- Obvious problems at KAD are poor standard of pipe maintenance, poor design.
- Cost of cleaning river could be £100,000.
- No other factories in the area use chlorine or bleaching agents.
- Many people want the plant closed down.

YOU:

- **don't like the chemicals industry**

- **support your paper's campaign on environmental protection, sponsored by environmental pressure groups**

- **know that many of your readers oppose the factory – but many others work there.**

YOU START.

44 PRODUCT ENDORSEMENT

(Negotiating; forecasting; urging)

When famous people endorse products, they say in advertisements that they approve of them and encourage people to buy them.

You are promotional director for a leading manufacturer of sports and fashion footwear. You are going to have a meeting with the agent (your partner) who represents Christina Wahlström, a rising young Swedish tennis star. You are interested in the possibility of her endorsing a new line of tennis shoe which you wish to promote.

You know that:

- Christina Wahlström is 17
- is coached by her father
- has reached the quarter finals at Wimbledon and the semi-finals of the Australian Open
- has already attracted a lot of press coverage because of her fiery temper on and off court. You are worried that she would create a bad image for your products.

Your product:

- is a new tennis shoe in a range of pastel colours which you want to promote heavily in the teenage market
- incorporates a revolutionary new kind of sole which gives extra bounce, lift and speed of turn. (Tests are not yet complete but you are keen to rush the product to market in time for the new season)
- is very expensive, so you want the endorsement of someone with whom teenagers will identify strongly.

YOU:

- **are ready to sign a deal worth $1/2m with the right person**

- **want reassurance about Wahlström's image**

- **don't want to talk too much about how long it will take to complete the tests on the product.**

Persuade your partner of your views.

YOUR PARTNER WILL START.

 © Penguin Books 1996

(Obliging; expressing fear/worry; urging)

Production delays can be caused by many factors from the non-delivery of parts to planning mistakes. The consequences can be small, such as a little internal disruption, or considerable, such as loss of important business.

You are production manager for a Portuguese electronic components manufacturer. One of your major customers is your parent company, DGS Holdings. You recently sent them the fax below.

EUSEBIO TORRES S.A.
PASO DO TOQUINHO 200
TORRES VEDRAS
007893 PORTUGAL

FAX: 351 61 324288
TEL: 351 61 567344

FOR THE ATTENTION OF: Robin Keeler, DGS Holdings – Production Dept.

MESSAGE

I am sorry to report that the order dated May 22 for a consignment of part numbers DR 56821 and TR 55901 has been delayed due to production problems. We cannot ship the parts on June 10 as requested. Delay by three weeks, to July 1.

We regret the inconvenience this may cause.

Best regards,

Maria Pinto   Luis Deias

Maria Pinto and Luis Deias

The production department at DGS contacts you to ask for an explanation.

YOU:

- do not want DGS to visit you because there are many problems at the plant which you would prefer to resolve alone

- know that there have been problems since a very popular senior worker was sacked for stealing an electric drill

- do not want to admit it, but there is a strike on at the moment

- know that the plant lost a major local customer last week and that any further loss of business would be a disaster

- fear that the management would be reorganized if DGS send a team to Portugal to investigate

- could suggest a top level internal inquiry to resolve problems.

YOUR PARTNER WILL START.

                    © Penguin Books 1996

A profit and loss account is a statement of income and expenditure for a business in a particular time period, normally one year. It shows trading performance in terms of what has been spent and what has been raised through sales and other revenue generating activities.

At the end of the financial year, you telephone a colleague at a sister company to ask for details of his/her company's profit and loss account. Your companies operate in the property, retailing and leisure sectors.

Ask for information to complete the missing information in the abbreviated profit and loss account shown below.

YEAR TO 31 MARCH 19—		*Previous year*
Trading surplus (before depreciation)	. . . . . .	(9.5m)
Income from property	. . . . . .	(4.6m)
Less: depreciation	. . . . . .	(3.5m)
Pre-interest profits	. . . . . .	(10.6m)
Less: interest payments	. . . . . .	(3.4m)
Pre-tax profits	. . . . . .	(7.2m)
Less: tax	. . . . . .	(2.3m)
Available to shareholders	. . . . . .	(4.9m)

YOU:

- **want to know reasons for the fall in profit**

- **wonder if empty property should be sold**

- **want to know what the prospects are for next year**

- **are surprised by the figure for interest payments and ask for an explanation**

- **want to know your colleague's assessment of the company's performance**

- **are personally very worried about the trend, especially in the light of market conditions**

- **would like to know more about competitors' performance.**

YOU START.

47 PROJECT MANAGEMENT

(Agreeing/disagreeing; judging; measuring and calculating)

Project management is an important business activity which involves putting plans into practice. It requires the coordination of various activities, each within a specified time frame.

You have recently been made assistant to the project leader in a project to build a new £2m production site. Your boss has presented you with the following outline schedule. He/she asks for your comments and/or approval of the schedule.

Week	Phase	Action
6–7	I	Setting objectives
		Establishing definitions
		Establishing specifications
8–9	II	Organization
		Deciding project leaders and teams
10	III	Cost estimating and budgeting
11	IV	Putting out to tender
12–15	V	Detailed discussions
16–18	VI	Deciding on allocation of work
		Meetings with tenderers
19	VII	Contracts
20–21	VIII	Planning and scheduling
22–24	IX	Construction I: Site preparation
25–28	X	Construction II: Foundations
29–34	XI	Construction III: Above-ground structure
35–38	XII	Finishing work

© Penguin Books 1996

YOU:

- think there are many serious problems with this schedule
- think it is impossible to say how many weeks the actual construction will take
- think it is even more impossible to divide the time required for the construction into accurate forecasts
- are an experienced geologist and you think that only after surveys of the site can estimates be made for the time required to build the foundations
- are sure that the exact time required for the building will depend on who wins the contract – and that will not be decided for four months
- think the site could be prepared before the contracts are awarded – and could be done concurrently with any other stage, so saving 2–3 weeks
- think that site preparation does not have to be done by the main contractor
- feel strongly about all the above, but you do not want to upset your boss right at the beginning of a project that you will have to see through together.

YOUR PARTNER WILL START.

(Agreeing/disagreeing; judging)

Quality improvement is the process of improving all the systems and procedures within your organization so that you produce better goods or services for your customers. Quality is not an absolute. The quality of your goods and services is defined by what your customers expect.

Your company has asked you and your partner to draw up a list of proposals for improving quality within your organization(s).

Select six of the following which you both feel should definitely form part of your company's new commitment to total quality:

- appointment of quality control inspectors for random checks on finished goods ☐
- creation of quality circles throughout the company ☐
- establishment of a regular quality competition with prizes for best suggestions for improving quality and saving money ☐
- introduction of a regular quality feature in the in-house magazine ☐
- decision to seek international quality standard (e.g. ISO 9000) ☐
- drafting of a quality charter to be sent to all customers ☐
- creation of telephone hotlines so that customers can get immediate help with problems and give immediate feedback on your products/services ☐
- introduction of a quality improvement training programme for all staff members ☐
- appointment of a top manager to have overall responsibility for the quality improvement programme ☐
- the establishment of quality targets (zero defects) in production ☐
- the prominent display of quality notices throughout the company buildings. ☐

Is there anything else you might like to add?

YOU START.

   © Penguin Books 1996

(Questioning)

Quizzes are usually fairly light-hearted but they can also tell us quite interesting things about ourselves and about other people.

Ask your partner the following business quiz questions and then get him/her to ask you. You can either answer each question in turn or each of you can go through the whole list in turn.

1 Do you work mainly:
   a) for money?
   b) for power?
   c) for fame?
   d) for self esteem?

2 If you won a lot of money, would you:
   a) invest it in your company?
   b) start your own company?
   c) retire?
   d) spend it?

3 If someone asked you how much you earned, would you:
   a) tell them the right figure?
   b) tell them the wrong figure?
   c) ask them to reply to the same question first?
   d) refuse to tell them?

4 Which is most important for you in your work:
   a) chances to meet people?
   b) friendly colleagues?
   c) a sympathetic boss?
   d) a good physical working environment?

5 If you found your new boss very difficult, would you:
   a) try to discuss the problem with him/her?
   b) try to tolerate the situation?
   c) ask for a transfer to another department?
   d) leave the company?

6 In meetings, do you normally:
   a) say less than the others?
   b) say more than the others?
   c) say as much as the others?
   d) chair the meeting?

7 In your opinion, should the average business meeting last:
   a) no more than an hour?
   b) no more than an hour and a half?
   c) no more than two hours?
   d) as long as it takes to complete the business properly?

8 Do people in your company normally arrive at a meeting:
   a) before or on time?
   b) less than five minutes late?
   c) between five and ten minutes late?
   d) more than ten minutes late?

9 Which of the following would most increase your own productivity at work:
   a) more autonomy?
   b) more time?
   c) more computers?
   d) more money?

YOUR PARTNER WILL START.

© Penguin Books 1996

(Questioning)

Ask your partner the following business quiz questions and then get him/her to ask you. You can either answer each question in turn or each of you can go through the whole list in turn.

1 Do you socialize with colleagues outside work time:
   a) often?
   b) sometimes?
   c) occasionally?
   d) never?

2 If your boss told you that you were wanted to represent your company on a stand at a trade fair for five days, would the prospect:
   a) excite you?
   b) horrify you?
   c) frighten the life out of you? or
   d) would you ask for extra money?

3 Which is most important to you in your work:
   a) your telephone?
   b) your computer?
   c) your fax machine?
   d) your desk?

4 In your opinion, should your company be:
   a) research-driven?
   b) product-driven?
   c) market-driven?
   d) customer-driven?

5 How many days' holiday (including public holidays) do you think people should take off work per year:
   a) fewer than 15?
   b) between 16 and 25?
   c) between 26 and 35?
   d) more than 35?

6 How much time do you normally take for lunch at work:
   a) less than 30 minutes?
   b) 30–60 minutes?
   c) 60–90 minutes?
   d) more than 90 minutes?

7 Do you think an employee should be sacked if caught in the workplace:
   a) stealing?
   b) smoking in a no-smoking area?
   c) taking drugs?
   d) sexually harassing a colleague?
      (You may wish to choose more than one.)

8 Do you prefer to be paid:
   a) a high base salary with no fringe benefits and no performance-related bonus?
   b) a low base salary with good fringe benefits?
   c) a low base salary with performance-related bonus?
   d) a low base salary with performance-related bonus and fringe benefits?

9 Do you prefer to work:
   a) mostly in an office?
   b) mostly at home?
   c) mostly travelling around?
   d) a mixture of working at the office, at home, and travelling around?

YOUR PARTNER WILL START.

 © Penguin Books 1996

(Questioning; forecasting)

Companies can raise extra finance to help meet their needs in several ways. Three examples are by a flotation (the sale of shares), a rights issue (selling shares at a special low price to existing shareholders), or taking out a loan from a bank through a mortgage or debenture.

You are a financial consultant. You have been asked to look at the accounts of a company called Chapman Whitney Ltd. They want to invest in new plant to meet expansion plans. You have a meeting with a representative of the company to discuss ways to raise extra finance.

Ask the representative of the company for:

- **an assessment of the world market**
- **an assessment of the present trading performance and future prospects for Chapman Whitney.**

Here is the company balance sheet for the last financial year.

SOURCES OF FINANCE		$m
Share capital 4 million shares at $1.0		4.0
Retained profits		8.0
Shareholders' funds		12.0
Debt finance		
6% mortgage (3 years)	6.0	
Bank overdraft	4.0	10.0
Total funds		**22.0**
Assets employed		
Fixed assets		
Property	10.0	
Machinery	2.0	
Vehicles	2.0	14.0
Net current assets		8.0
Total assets		**22.0**

Fig. 1 Chapman Whitney Ltd. Abbreviated balance sheet.

YOU:

- **think expansion should be made only if at least one of the following conditions are met:**
  a) expanding world market
  b) increasing market share

- **think shareholders will not want to invest more in Chapman Whitney – unless the above two conditions apply**

- **think the present level of borrowing (see Fig. 1) is too high – almost 50% of total assets.**

YOUR PARTNER WILL START.

(Liking and preferring; urging; declining/rejecting)

Recruitment is the process of looking for and finding people to do particular jobs. Recruitment can be a time-consuming and costly process. Recruiting the wrong person can be a very expensive mistake.

You are the business partner of an American up-market designer of men's clothes, running your own medium-sized company. He/she (your partner) provides the creative inspiration and you look after the business side of things. You have a good working relationship. Your company has traditionally operated in the US and is now trying to break into the European market. Your partner is based in New York and you have been in Paris for three months. You are phoning each other (at 10.00 French time, 17.00 US time) to decide which candidate should get the new job of sales and marketing manager for France (and potentially for the whole of Europe). Each of you has shortlisted two candidates whom you have personally interviewed. Unfortunately your partner's fax machine is not working, so you have to describe your own shortlisted candidates to your partner over the phone.

1 **Read the two profiles below and decide which of your own two candidates you prefer.**
2 **Describe them both to your partner.**
3 **State your own recommendation.**
4 **Persuade your partner of the advantages of your preferred candidate.**

YOU:

- strongly favour a European choice because you feel that a European will penetrate the European market much more quickly and successfully than an outsider.

Name	Yves de Lalaubie
Age	31
Nationality	French
Marital status	Engaged (for 3 years)
Education	MBA from prestigious HEC, Paris (one year at Stanford as part of his French MBA course)
Experience	Marketing position with major French men's fashion house (2 years) before founding own 'fashion broking' consultancy which was bankrupted four years later during the recession – attracted lots of attention in the specialized media
Languages	Native French, fluent Italian, English passable but by no means fluent.
Salary expectation	Asking for 20% over the upper figure we agreed
Interests	Paris night life
Other relevant information	A well-known younger figure on the French fashion circuit. Lots of contacts. Thinks Paris fashion is dead and that new marketing techniques will revolutionize the way people buy clothes. Rumoured to have very right-wing views

© Penguin Books 1996

Name	Ashley Ryedale
Age	29
Nationality	British
Marital status	Single
Education	Architecture at Cambridge and MBA from INSEAD (European business school near Paris) just completed
Experience	3 years in architecture before moving to Paris for personal reasons. 2 years in a marketing job in the travel business led him to do the MBA. Glowing reference from former employer: 'he made a significant impact on our figures, he has brilliant marketing intuition'
Languages	Native English, fluent French, and varying degrees of command of Italian, Spanish, German and Dutch. Currently learning Hungarian
Salary expectation	Reasonable
Interests	Art and architecture, theatre, music, literature, history of fashion.
Other relevant information	Quiet, discreet, good talker, great sense of humour. Genuinely enthusiastic about our designs. Wants a job combining aesthetic with business interest. Declared openly at the interview that he is homosexual: does not have established relationship with one partner

YOUR PARTNER WILL START.

53 RECYCLING

(Agreeing/disagreeing; judging)

Recycling is the activity of sorting out waste material so that it can be reprocessed by specialist companies. Recycling is broadly considered to be a sensible way to reduce the exploitation of the environment.

Your company produces 25,000 tons of waste products from its offices and canteen areas every year. At present there is no policy on recycling and you think there should be one.

Together with a colleague, decide on the three most important advantages of recycling and whether there are any important disadvantages. Then decide if you want to recommend the formal introduction of procedures on recycling and any related considerations.

YOU:

- **think there is good public relations value in recycling**
- **think recycling will reduce the amount of rubbish**
- **fear that you will have to deal with various different recycling companies**
- **believe the volume of paper used could be reduced by using more electronic mail**
- **think the company should only buy recycled paper products.**

YOUR PARTNER WILL START.

© Penguin Books 1996

54 RELOCATION

Student B

(Judging; negotiating)

Relocation means moving your home, office or factory from one place to another.

You are the manager of a new joint venture whose head office is in Brussels. You are busy recruiting a number of people from all over Europe, including people from two parent companies. You are keen to recruit one European manager (your partner) but you have strong reservations about his/her refusal to relocate from his/her own country: all your other recruits have agreed to move. He/she proposes to commute to Brussels on a weekly basis, travelling in on Monday morning and out on Friday evening each week.

YOU:

- **feel you cannot treat one member of the team differently from the others**
- **think that paying the weekly air fare will be very expensive**
- **believe that too much travelling is bad for productivity.**

However, you are keen to have him/her on the team. Discuss the question with your new employee at a meeting. You must reach an agreement. Although you want your partner on the team, you will not sacrifice your company's interests to keep him/her.

YOU START.

(Measuring and calculating; correcting)

When you fix sales targets, you predict the quantity of goods or services you will sell during a future time period.

Your company's sales operation is divided into a number of regions, and you and your partner have joint responsibility for the Central region: you manage the East Central area and your partner manages the West Central area.

Last year the company's management announced a new incentive scheme for sales staff: the winning sales team would win a week's holiday in the Caribbean for themselves and their spouses. Although you made big efforts to sell more than the other regions, you saw the other teams pulling ahead of you. In addition, computer problems made you late with the figures for the last quarter of the year.

Your computer manager now tells you that some of the original figures for your area are wrong: the new figures are on the whole higher than you thought.

1 **Calculate your new total sales for the year.**

2 **Call your opposite number in West Central and see if, together, your figures are now good enough to win the prize.**

Figures in $US	North	West	South	East
First quarter	93,137	94,005	85,211	93,140
Second quarter	101,104	98,276	85,439	99,505
Third quarter	103,721	99,422	87,624	102,099
Fourth quarter			89,423	102,600
Total				

Figures in $US	West Central Initial	West Central Revised	East Central Initial	East Central Revised	Central Revised Total
First quarter	46,010		47,194	47,668	
Second quarter	48,763		51,309	51,309	
Third quarter	49,345		51,499	51,699	
Fourth quarter	49,557		51,446	50,230	
Total					

YOUR PARTNER WILL START.

© Penguin Books 1996

56 SMALL TALK 1

Student B

(Welcoming; greetings and farewells; introducing self)

Small talk is a vital skill in business. It can be difficult to initiate a conversation and then to keep it going, but it is very important to be able to do so – in English as well as in your own language.

1   You are a visitor to a company where you have an appointment with the CEO (chief executive officer).

YOUR PARTNER WILL START.

2   A visitor to your company is waiting to see your CEO and you have been asked to look after him/her for ten minutes. It is your job to keep the conversation going.

Spend ten minutes talking to the visitor. While you are talking, try to direct the conversation so that the visitor uses as many of the words below as possible. At the end of ten minutes, count up how many of the words in the box below he/she used.

```
FEEL / FLIGHT / SLOW / PICTURE / CARRY /
CITY / BEACH / SIT / RED
```

YOU START.

(Introducing self; questioning; expressing amazement)

Fill in the form below to invent a new identity for yourself!

> Name: ....
>
> Nationality: ....
>
> Age: ....
>
> Address: ....
>
> Company: ....
>
> Company activity: ....
>
> Position: ....
>
> Responsibilities: ....
>
> Length of service: ....
>
> Current trip to: ....
>
> Reason: ....
>
> Family: ....
>
> Interests: ....
>
> Other information: ....

Now imagine that the 'new you' is sitting in a plane next to another business traveller and that you begin to talk. Tell the other person (your partner) as much as possible about yourself. And find out as much as possible about your partner.

YOUR PARTNER WILL START.

© Penguin Books 1996

(Obliging; regretting; measuring and calculating)

Parts, or components, are put together in manufacturing or assembly processes to make products, or are used to replace faulty or damaged parts in existing products.

Your company is a successful manufacturer of high precision metal components. A customer calls you with a surprise order.

The following is a computer print-out of stock and availability for the goods required.

Part Number	In stock	Shortest possible delivery time
FR4001	1432	immediate delivery up to 600 + 3 days for every additional 200
FR4002	250	immediate delivery up to 100 + 7 days for every additional 200
GA20	200	7 days for up to 100 + 2 days for every additional 100
GA25	300	7 days for up to 50 + 2 days for every additional 50
HK287	600	immediate delivery up to 300 + 7 days for every additional 100
HK320	850	immediate delivery up to 250 + 7 days for every additional 100
HT10	2750	immediate delivery up to 1000 + 7 days for every additional 500
XT10	950	immediate delivery up to 300 + 7 days for every additional 300

YOU:

- **cannot allow stocks to fall below 50 for any product**
- **can offer to supply part of an order when your stocks do not allow you to meet a whole order**
- **know that the caller is an important customer but you have other large customers placing regular orders that you must meet**
- **can offer to supply some of the above parts before the requested date**
- **cannot improve on the availability situation described above**
- **could offer slightly sub-standard products to meet additional requirements for FR products**
- **would prefer not to offer any discount on such short notice orders – but use your judgement in this case**
- **will invoice at the time of delivery, with payment at 60 days from delivery.**

YOUR PARTNER WILL START.

(Liking and preferring; judging)

More and more work is project work and more and more project work is done in teams. In the future, you could be a member of several teams working on several different projects at the same time. Team members play different but equally important roles and a good team is one with a good balance between roles.

You and your partner are forming a special team to work on a major new project. You are looking for two other people to join you to form a dynamic and balanced team.

Look at the brief descriptions of team roles below. A well-balanced team will have people with different preferences situated in different places on the wheel.

Reporter-Advisers gain information before taking action; interpret situations and give advice.

Creator-Innovators find new ideas and approaches; research; explore the future.

Explorer-Promoters look for new opportunities; find new contacts and resources; promote and sell ideas.

Assessor-Developers make ideas work in practice; develop prototypes and test plans.

Thruster-Organizers make things happen; organize what has to be done; ensure objectives are met.

Concluder-Producers carry things through; work to orderly plans and systems; meet deadlines.

Controller-Inspectors control processes; inspect standards; ensure procedures are followed.

Upholder-Maintainers clarify purpose, values and principles; provide support; maintain standards.

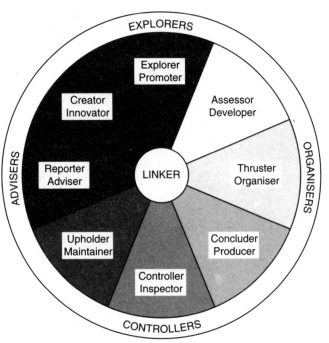

Margerison-McCann
TEAM MANAGEMENT WHEEL

The Team Management Wheel and role descriptions were developed by Charles Margerison and Dick McCann of Team Management Systems UK Ltd.

The Margerison-McCann Team Management Wheel is a registered trademark of Prado Systems Ltd. For precise pinpointing of a person's preferred role, it is necessary to complete the Team Management Index, a questionnaire developed by Margerison and McCann, which also provides a detailed personal profile for reference during discussions aimed at improving teamwork.

Discuss with your partner:

• **which role you think you would prefer to play in the team**

• **which role your partner would prefer to play**

• **which other two roles you need to make a balanced team.**

YOUR PARTNER WILL START.

© Penguin Books 1996

(Blaming; agreeing/disagreeing; urging)

Managing your time well is one of the most important skills that anyone in business can learn. If you do not, the results are frustration for yourself and your colleagues, and loss of money for your company.

First of all, your partner is going to tell you about four typical time management problems. Look at the list below and tell him or her which you think is the solution to each problem. Add your own comments.

> **The solutions**
>
> a Give subordinates more autonomy so that they don't feel the need to check with you all the time. Teach people that a closed door means that you should not be disturbed. Tell everyone that there are certain fixed times of day when you need to work on your own.
>
> b Hire a full-time technical consultant with unlimited patience and an unlimited willingness to explain. Spend three times as much money on technical training as you do at the moment.
>
> c Get the receptionist or a secretary to screen your calls or, if you have a direct line, install an answering machine and switch it on when you don't want to be interrupted.
>
> d Always be clear when each meeting is supposed to finish. Don't have a meeting just because it's the weekly meeting, even if there's nothing to discuss. Don't tolerate discussion between two people which is of no concern to the others present. Decide how much time you should spend in meetings and then count how much time you do spend in meetings. If the first figure is smaller than the second, then do everything you can to bring the second figure down.

Now it's your turn to tell your partner about four common problems experienced by people who have difficulty managing their time. Listen to the solutions which he or she recommends and add your own comments.

> **The problems**
>
> 1 People don't understand that my time is valuable and not to be wasted.
> 2 My desk is a mess.
> 3 People are always dropping into my office to chat.
> 4 I work very hard but there always seems to be even more work piling up.

YOUR PARTNER WILL START.

61 TRAINING PRIORITIES

(Knowing; agreeing/disagreeing; sequencing)

Prioritizing is deciding on an order of importance for a number of possible actions, by comparing their usefulness. The most useful are often urgently required, while the least useful may be disregarded.

Your company produces high quality audio equipment for use by professional sound engineers in the music, film and television industries. You are planning a major sales and marketing drive in several new export markets in Europe and Asia. You are the new marketing director with responsibility for this major initiative and your colleague is another senior executive of the company.

Together with your colleague, set priorities for training a staff of five marketing managers and 20 sales representatives and agents.

Decide on an order of one to nine, eliminating the lowest three or four areas of training – depending on your assessment of their value.

- foreign language training for reps and agents in the countries concerned ☐
- foreign language training for your five marketing managers ☐
- training in cultural awareness for five marketing managers ☐
- training in developing new markets and marketing strategy for your colleague, the Marketing Director ☐
- training in marketing strategy for reps and agents ☐
- training in new product technology and after-sales service for reps and agents ☐
- training in new product technology and after-sales service for marketing managers ☐
- training in new support software for marketing campaigns for marketing managers ☐
- production of detailed guidelines for sales reps and agents in various languages. ☐

YOUR PARTNER WILL START.

 © Penguin Books 1996

62 TRANSPORTATION

Student B

(Judging; agreeing/disagreeing)

Distribution is concerned with moving goods from the producer to the customer.

Your company wants to export goods from Spain to Greece. You are based in Spain and have obtained information on the most appropriate way of moving 120 tons of goods to Greece every month. Contact your colleague to discuss your proposal.

YOU:

- think reliability is more important than price
- think speedy delivery is less important than regular delivery (the goods must arrive in the first week of every month)
- want your company to be as independent as possible and to handle all documentation
- think your company should use its own export department to arrange transport through a Barcelona shipping company, Puig Hernandez S.A.
- know that Puig Hernandez runs a regular merchant shipping service from Barcelona to Athens with departures every Monday and Thursday
- understand that the voyage takes four days
- want onward delivery in Greece to be co-ordinated with the Greek haulage company Halkos S.A., already regular partners to your company with a fleet of 40 lorries
- have obtained the following cost estimates:
  Per month $18,000 for 120 tons of goods + road haulage $7,000.

YOU START.

63 WORK ENVIRONMENT

Student B

(Negotiating; measuring and calculating; forecasting)

The working environment has long been recognized as a key factor in improving productivity, employee satisfaction and in reducing days lost through sickness.

You work in a telesales office with eight sales staff, for a company with a turnover of £1.25m. You are an employees' representative responsible for health and safety. You believe that several factors make the office old-fashioned and uncomfortable – and even bad for the health of your colleagues.

YOU:

- **feel that an improvement in the working conditions would result in higher productivity, happier staff and fewer days off for reasons of minor illness**

- **think the company turnover easily justifies major improvements in the working environment**

- **know the company has spent almost nothing on the office for five years.**

You have drawn up the note below about working conditions:

- The work stations – old-fashioned and uncomfortable
- Desks – wrong height – drawers hard to open
- Chairs – bad design
- Lighting causes headaches
- Paintwork – dull, depressing
- Traffic noise from the street
- Cold in winter – too hot in summer
- The space is too small.

You have a meeting with a manager responsible for the office. Ask for improvements in as many areas as you can.

YOUR PARTNER WILL START.

170 © Penguin Books 1996

64 WORK ROTAS

(Regretting; declining/rejecting; agreeing/disagreeing)

Holiday entitlement is established in employees' contracts but the exact time when holidays are taken is usually negotiated between the company and the individuals concerned. The company naturally has to make sure that there is sufficient cover when employees are away on holiday.

You are a line supervisor in a foods production company. You are also a parent with children at school. You are pleased that your own holiday this year coincides with the children's school holiday – and your partner's holiday.

Here is your calendar showing your holiday plans:

	week	M	T	W	T	F	S/S
JULY	27	4	5	6	7	8	9/10
	28	11	12	13	(14) School holidays start	15	16 (17) Leave for USA
	29	18	19	20	21	22	23/24
	30	25	26	27	28	29	30 (31) return
AUGUST	31	1	2	3	4	5	6/7
	32	8	9	10	11	12	13/14
	33	15	16	17	18	19	20/21
	34	22	23	24	25	26	27/28
	35	29	30	31	1	2	3/4
SEPTEMBER	36	5	(6) School starts	7	8	9	10/11

Holiday California USA !!!

YOU:

- **would like promotion to a higher grade in your company**
- **and your family have not had a real holiday for three years and this one is already booked.**

YOUR PARTNER WILL START.

© Penguin Books 1996

171

65 WORKS COUNCIL

Student B

(Urging; agreeing/disagreeing; hesitating)

Many companies in the industrialized world have works councils: committees of representatives of both management and staff which meet regularly. However, the powers of works councils can vary widely from country to country and from company to company. In Germany and Scandinavia, for example, employees' representatives may participate in decisions about the company's financial, marketing and human resources strategy. Elsewhere, the works council may have a much more limited role.

You and your partner serve on the works council of the medium-sized company where you both work. The company employs 100 people. Each year the council is given a £5,000 Christmas present by the company's owners to spend in whatever way it wishes. You and your partner are meeting to brainstorm your ideas before the full council meeting to discuss the subject. You have jotted the following ideas down on the back of an envelope. Compare your notes with your partner's and try to reach a joint decision on what you would like to recommend. (You can add your own ideas to the list below.)

YOU think the money could go on:

- a Christmas party for all staff accompanied by husbands and wives: buffet dinner, free drinks, live band and entertainment

- the purchase of part of one share in the company per employee

- the donation of the entire sum to the company musical society. It has ambitious plans to stage a production of *Evita* next year but cannot yet go ahead because of a shortage of funds

- a contribution to the works council fund set up to buy a chalet in a holiday resort for the use of staff members at a subsidized rate

- your own ideas.

YOU START.

© Penguin Books 1996

Glossary

Abolish   Get rid of, stop, ban.

Absenteeism   Being away from work, usually through sickness; a measure of the number of people away from work.

Accounts   Figures giving information about what a company earns and spends, how much profit it makes, and so on.

Acknowledgement   A short letter to tell someone who has written to you that you have received his/her letter.

Acquisition   The purchase of one company by another.

Agenda   A list of points to discuss in a meeting. The agenda also gives other important information like the list of people who will be at the meeting, the date and place, and the starting and finishing times.

Appraise   Measure the performance of someone, give feedback on the performance of someone.

Assault   Physical attack.

Assets   Things owned by a company which have value: property and saleable equipment, cash, finished goods, stock or saleable financial investments.

Audit   A detailed analysis of an important feature of an organization. Auditors – the people who carry out audits – usually write reports and make recommendations for changes to be made. Examples: a financial audit, a management audit, a language audit.

Autonomy   Independence, freedom to work on your own and to take important decisions affecting your work.

Balance sheet   A statement showing the financial position of a company at a particular time

Bankrupt   A company goes bankrupt when it has to stop doing business because of the size of its debts.

Bonus   A special extra payment.

Brainstorm   Write down as many possible solutions to a problem that you can think of before analysing the merits of each one in more detail. Brainstorming is usually a group activity.

Brand   A name or a symbol used for a product or service or range of products or services provided by a particular company, e.g. Coca-Cola, IBM, Hertz.

Breakthrough   A big development or new opportunity which could open the way to future success.

Bribe   An illegal payment made to get special treatment.

Briefing   Giving information to one or more people.

Broking   A broker is someone with specialist knowledge in a certain area who acts as a go-between (or 'middle man') between the customer and the supplier of products or services, for example an investment broker, an insurance broker. Broking is the activity.

Campaign   A plan which operates over a period of time in order to increase public or consumer awareness of a product or service, e.g. an advertising campaign.

Cash   Coins and banknotes; money which is available to spend immediately.

Cash balance   The amount of available cash in a company at a certain point in time. Cash budgets show an opening cash balance at the start of a period and a closing cash balance at the end.

Cash budget   A financial planning tool consisting of a description of income and expenditure over a certain period.

Cashflow The relationship between money received (sales) and money going out (costs).

Chargehand A low level position of non-managerial responsibility, a chargehand is in charge of a small group of workers. Chargehands report to supervisors.

Commute Travel from home to work and from work to home.

Conform Do or be the same as everyone else.

Contractor An independent company contracted to carry out specific work for another company at an agreed fee.

Convention A usual way of doing things, a habit.

Corporate hospitality The wining and dining of clients or potential clients at sporting or cultural events.

Corporate planning Major planning and development concerns within a company, such as new product areas, new markets, image building, marketing and financial goals.

Corrupt Doing business illegally for your own advantage is corrupt.

Cost of sales All costs involved in preparing a product or service for sale up to the actual sale itself. These include fixed overheads (rent, heating, wages and salaries) and variable costs (raw materials, overtime payments).

Cost of selling The cost of all promotional activities including advertising, sales commissions, fees to agents and distributors, distribution, storage and transport.

Counselling Confidential support and advice given to an individual with professional or personal problems.

Counselling service A service for giving advice to employees on personal or work-related problems.

Courtesy The treatment of other people with politeness and respect.

Creditor Someone to whom money is owed.

Current assets Assets used by a company in its daily work, such as materials, finished goods and cash.

Deadline The date or time by which you must complete a certain piece of work.

Debenture An agreement to pay back a loan at a fixed interest rate.

Debtor Someone who owes money.

Delegate Give work to a subordinate which you would otherwise do yourself.

Delivery Getting the goods physically to the customer.

Depreciation A notional sum appearing as an expense on a profit and loss account to spread the cost of capital assets over several years rather than appearing as a single expenditure at the time of purchase.

Discount A percentage or amount taken off the standard price.

Double glazing Windows with two layers of glass.

Downturn A period of falling sales or profits.

Etiquette Forms of polite behaviour.

Fixed assets Property or machinery which a company uses.

Flexibility Readiness to adapt to changing conditions.

Flotation The selling of shares in order to raise capital.

Found a company Start a company.

Franchise A licence to trade using a brand name in return for the payment of fees. The owner of the brand name is the franchisor who gives licences to franchisees. The more money franchisees make, the more they pay in fees.

Franchisee Someone who pays a royalty in order to trade using the name of a franchisor.

Fringe benefits Other advantages earned by an employee in addition to salary, for example a company car.

Funding   Money.

Funds transfer   An operation carried out by a bank to direct money from one company's account to another company's account.

Graduate (noun)   Someone who has completed a university course and who has received a university degree.

Handling charge   A fee charged for carrying out a service, especially as an intermediary or 'middleman'.

Haulage   Road transport of goods by lorry.

Haulier   Road transport company or trucking company.

Implement   Put a policy or plan into practice.

Incentive   Something to encourage employees to behave in a particular way, for example to work harder.

Invoice   A formal request for payment.

Itinerary   A programme for a trip or a visit, showing the order of events and the time of different activities.

Job-sharing   Where two employees divide a single job between them, so both work part-time.

Joint venture   An agreement between two or more companies to cooperate in an area such as research, product development, marketing, etc.

Jot   Write down notes.

Junk mail   Advertising material, often unwanted, sent by post to selected potential customers.

Just-in-time   Manufacturing companies with a just-in-time management system order components and materials so that they arrive at the factory just before they are needed. In this way they keep stocks low and so keep costs down.

Launch   The presentation of a new product on the first official day of its existence.

Lay off   To sack workers, temporarily or permanently.

(Take) legal advice   Talk to your lawyer.

Loan   Money borrowed for a specific purpose, usually from a bank.

(On) location   Working on a film outside a film studio.

Logistics   A general label for planning and operations, and sometimes computing activities.

Maternity leave   Time off work for a woman to have a baby.

Merger   When two companies join together under common ownership and management.

Morale   The general level of satisfaction of the workforce.

Mortgage   When an individual or company borrows money and pays back capital and interest. If the borrower cannot repay the money, the lender can take a property asset belonging to the borrower instead.

Net profit margin   The profit after tax, expressed as a figure or as a percentage of turnover.

Overdraft   Money borrowed from a bank on which interest is paid.

PA   Personal Assistant.

Pension   The money you receive from your company or from the State when you retire.

Performance-related   A system relating (usually some of) your pay to how well you work. The performance-related part of your pay is linked to how far you achieve an objective agreed by you and your superior.

Premises   An office or factory building.

Prioritize   Put things into an order of importance.

Productivity   The amount you produce and the efficiency with which you produce it.

Promotional literature   Leaflets, brochures, etc. advertising a product or service and describing its advantages.

Pull one's weight   Work as hard as one's colleagues; take a fair share of a responsibility.

Purchase   Buy.

Quality circle   A group of employees who meet regularly to discuss ways of improving the way they work and the quality of the goods or services they help to provide.

Questionnaire   A set of questions designed to find out information about people's attitudes, beliefs or opinions.

Quota   A defined and limited number.

Rating   A score on a scale, a measure.

Recession   A period (technically of three successive quarters) during which a national economy gets smaller.

Recruit (noun)   Someone starting a job with the company.

Redeemed   Paid back, especially a loan over a fixed time period such as a mortgage.

Redundancy   Loss of job, usually because the company cannot afford to continue to employ the person in the job.

Reference   A written or spoken review of your professional abilities or personal capacities made to a potential employer by someone you know.

Refund   Pay back.

Refurbish   Repair and redecorate.

Representative, rep.   Someone who usually travels around trying to sell goods or services for a particular company, as in sales representative or sales rep.

Retirement   A person leaving the company because he/she has reached the retirement age – usually 60 or 65 – or because of ill health.

Rights issue   A method of raising finance where a company sells shares at a special low price to existing shareholders.

Run (a company)   Manage a company.

Sack   Dismiss someone from a job.

Sales budget   A description of planned expenditure for producing and selling a product.

Screen a call   When secretaries screen telephone calls, they only allow through the ones that they know are really important.

Self esteem   Your feelings about yourself. If you have high self esteem, you feel positive about yourself. If you have low self esteem, you feel negative about yourself or you feel that others feel negative about you.

Sexual harassment   Where one employee makes unwelcome sexual remarks to a colleague or behaves sexually towards them in an unwelcome way.

Share   A certificate given in exchange for investing money in a company and representing a partial ownership in the assets of the company. Shares are bought in the hope of earning dividends, paid out when a company performs well, or of making a profit from reselling the shares at a higher value if the company has been performing well.

Shareholder   Someone who owns shares in a company.

Shoestring budget   A very limited budget.

Sponsorship   Financial support for an artistic, sporting or cultural enterprise provided by a private company in exchange for advertising rights.

Stock   A store of materials, components or products.

Subsidiary   A company partly or wholly owned by another.

Subsidized   Paid for in part by someone else.

Supervisor   A lower management position, responsible for all the workers and activities in a production area. Supervisors normally report to department managers.

Task force   A (usually) small group of people with a special job to do (usually) in a limited period of time. A task force, unlike a committee, is expected to get things done.

Tender, put out to   To invite tenders for a specific project.

Tenderer   A company that submits a tender.

Trade union   The formal organization of a group of workers which aims to improve the wages and working conditions of its members.

Turnover   Income from sales.

Upgrade   Improve, bring up to date.

Up market   The expensive, luxury end of the market.

Warehouse   Where parts or finished goods are stocked.

A–Z of Language Functions

This glossary gives some exponents for key functions indicated after the activity title. It is intended only as a quick reference to the kind of language practice a particular activity might generate. Teachers may wish to elicit or provide further exponents of a specific function before beginning an activity.

Agreeing/disagreeing
I agree with you/that.
Up to a point, I agree with you/that.
(I'm afraid) I disagree with you/that.

Blaming
I think you have made a mistake.
You're responsible for . . .
You shouldn't have done/said that.

Correcting
I think you've made a mistake there. It's not . . .
That's not quite right. I said . . .

Declining/rejecting (an offer)
No, thanks.
I'm sorry but I can't.
I'm afraid that's unacceptable.
I couldn't possibly accept that.

Emphasizing
The following words add emphasis:
real(ly). e.g. that's *really* wonderful.
absolute(ly). e.g. it was an *absolute* miracle.
indeed. e.g. their service was very good *indeed*.

Forecasting
The goods *are sure to* arrive tomorrow.
The goods *are likely to* arrive tomorrow.
The goods *may* arrive tomorrow.
The goods *are unlikely to* arrive tomorrow.
The goods *can't possibly* arrive tomorrow.

Greetings and farewells

Greetings for first meeting	*Reply*
Hello, how do you do?	How do you do?
Nice to meet you.	Nice to meet you, too.

Greetings for second and subsequent meetings	*Reply*
Nice to see you again. How are you?	Very well, thanks. And you?
	Fine thanks. And you?
	Not too good, I'm afraid.
	Awful/dreadful/terrible (between friends).

Farewells	*Reply*
Nice meeting you (again).	Nice meeting you (again), too.

Hesitating
Actually, . . .
Basically, . . .
You see . . .
You know . . .
It's like this, you see . . .

Introducing self and others
May I introduce myself? My name's . . .
And may I introduce my colleagues? This is . . .

Judging
I'm convinced/sure/positive . . .
I think/believe/feel . . .
I tend to think . . .
I'm inclined to feel . . .

Knowing
I know we sent the goods.
I think we sent the goods.
I doubt if we sent the goods.

Liking and preferring
I like visiting clients. (= I enjoy it)
I like to visit clients in their offices. (= It is appopriate)
I prefer working in my office to travelling abroad.
I'd rather work in my office than travel abroad.

Measuring and calculating
If you add the figures together, you get . . .
If you take the total time and subtract . . ., you get . . .
Let's see what we get if we divide/multiply . . . by . . .

Negotiating
Let's discuss the terms of the contract.
I'd like to settle the disagreement between us.
I think we can accept this contract if you . . .

Obliging (see also vetoing)
1 *To be obliged to do something:*
We must find a way of solving the cashflow problems.
Do we have to do what he says? Isn't there an alternative?
2 *To oblige someone to do something:*
These cashflow problems require us to look at our payment policy.
(require/force/compel/oblige someone to do something)
The problems have made us re-evaluate our current practices.

Permitting
You may take as much time as you need.
We are allowed/permitted to claim travel expenses.
May/might I make a comment at this point?
Do you mind if I . . .?

Questioning

Could you tell me . . .?
I'd like to know . . .
I wonder if you could tell me . . .
Do you happen to know . . .?

Regretting

It's a (great) shame/pity that . . .
I'm sorry to hear that . . .
I'm afraid that . . .
Unfortunately, . . .

Sequencing

First/first of all/initially/to start with
Second/secondly
Then/after that/next/subsequently
Finally

Telling

I told him that . . .
I said (to him) that . . .
I informed them about . . .
I explained what/how/that . . .
I reported to them that . . .

Urging

We should make a decision soon.
You ought to review the situation.
I suggest that you check your records.
I (would) advise you to check your records.

Vetoing (see also obliging)

1 *To be obliged not to do something:*
You mustn't/may not give this information to anyone outside the
    company.
You are not allowed/permitted to . . .
2 *To oblige someone not to do something:*
The regulations prohibit us from giving this information to anyone
outside the company.

Welcoming

Welcome to . . .
It's a pleasure to welcome you to . . .
We are very pleased to have you with us.

(E)Xpressing Your amaZement (and other emotions)

Amazement
This is a surprise!
I'm very surprised that . . .
Fear / worry
I'm worried about . . .
I'm concerned that . . .

Gratitude
I'm very grateful to you for . . .
It was very kind of you to . . .
Sympathy
I'm very sorry about . . .
Indifference
It doesn't matter.
I don't mind.
I don't care.

Communication Skill Table

	Presentation	Phone call	Meeting/discussion	Negotiation	Social English
1 Ice breaker			x		x
2 Advertising			x	x	
3 Agendas		x			
4 Bank charges		x			
5 Budget presentation	x		x		
6 Business anecdote	x				
7 Business etiquette			x		x
8 Business gifts			x		
9 Business initials			x		
10 Buying and selling			x	x	
11 Cashflow problems			x	x	
12 Company of the year			x		
13 Company organization					
14 Company presentation	x				
15 Company tour	x				
16 Company visit		x			x
17 Corporate culture			x		
18 Corporate sponsorship			x	x	
19 Costs and reducing overheads			x		
20 Customer care			x		
21 Customer complaint		x	x	x	
22 Customs holdup		x	x	x	
23 Employee morale	x		x		
24 Entertaining visitors	x		x		x
25 Environmentally friendly office			x		
26 Equal opportunities			x		
27 Franchising				x	
28 Health and safety			x		
29 In-house magazine	x		x	x	

#	Item					
30	Interview techniques			x	x	
31	Job application			x		
32	Large versus small companies			x		
33	Late payment of invoice		x	x	x	
34	Management and leadership skills for women			x		
35	Management qualities			x		
36	Market research			x	x	
37	Market survey			x		
38	Meeting arrangements			x	x	
39	Mission statement			x		
40	Pay versus benefits		x	x		
41	Performance appraisal			x		
42	Presenting information					x
43	Press and public relations			x		
44	Product endorsement		x			
45	Production delays			x	x	
46	Profit and loss account			x	x	
47	Project management			x		
48	Quality			x		
49	Quiz 1			x		
50	Quiz 2			x		
51	Raising finance			x		
52	Recruitment			x	x	x
53	Recycling			x		
54	Relocation		x	x		
55	Sales targets					x
56	Small talk 1	x				
57	Small talk 2	x		x	x	
58	Spare parts		x		x	
59	Team building			x		
60	Time management			x		x
61	Training priorities			x		
62	Transportation				x	
63	Work environment		x	x		
64	Work rotas		x	x		
65	Works council		x	x		